M000095919

Contents

Introduction

The school curriculum designates the topics taught to students. Health is one of the subjects that teachers should target. However, most stress is put on the core subjects, which leaves little time for this important area. An increased interest in the health of Americans has led to a revised interest in promoting health in the classroom.

Research suggests that the greatest threats to the health of Americans today are lifestyle diseases, such as cardiovascular disease and cancer. Among children, injuries claim more lives than disease. The facts that determine the length and quality of an individual's life are most often personal choices in several areas: diet, exercise, and personal cleanliness; the use of tobacco, alcohol, and other drugs; and the application of new health information to one's own habits. Responsibility for maintaining health and for minimizing the risk of developing chronic and degenerative diseases and disorders rests with the individual and begins early in life.

To achieve this goal, health education should promote positive attitudes, consistent positive behaviors, and good decision-making skills, which will contribute to good health and long-range prevention of disease. Effective health education should combine content and skill practice in a meaningful way that is applicable to daily life. Thus, health education is really life education. *Health, Nutrition, and P.E.* provides content and skills practice that will benefit all children. The activity pages address health concepts that can be applied on a personal level.

Organization

Health, Nutrition, and P.E. is divided into three units.

- **Unit 1** provides information on growth, the body, hygiene, and drugs.
- **Unit 2** introduces information on nutrition. It includes background about the new food pyramid and healthy food selections.
- **Unit 3** explores fitness and exercise concepts. It offers activity pages explaining the benefits of exercise as well as specific, hands-on exercise suggestions.

Additional Notes

- **Correlation Chart** A correlation chart can be found on pages 3 and 4. At a glance, it can help you plan your curriculum to ensure that key health and physical education standards are being met.

- **Assessment** A three-page assessment is found on pages 5 through 7. You can use the test as a diagnostic tool by administering it before students begin the activities. After completing the activities, you may wish to test students again to gauge their progress.

- **Teacher Resource** Each unit begins with an introduction. It provides background information important to completing some of the skill pages and gives an overview of the concepts students will explore.

- **Bulletin Board** A bulletin board idea accompanies each unit. The idea is either student created or interactive, which meets standards required for classroom decoration. Detailed instructions explain how to build the board.

- **Science Project** Each unit contains a science project that could be used in a science fair.

Health, Nutrition, and P.E. 5–6, SV 1419023608

Standards Correlation Chart

Use this correlation chart to locate specific pages dealing with a listed skill.

Standards	Pages
Health	
Identifies the basic structure of the human body	Unit 1: most pages
Describes the different parts and functions of body systems	Unit 1: 17–54
Describes the structure and function of the eyes and ears	42, 43
Identifies healthful behaviors to care for body systems	26, 55–63
Identifies major glands and hormones of the endocrine system	48, 49
Explains how growth occurs	13, 48, 49, 50, 51
Describes changes in male and female anatomy and physiology during puberty	49
Describes how sleep, rest, and hygiene affect growth	55
Describes how traits are inherited	52, 53, 54
Identifies the importance of caring for teeth and gums	55
Identifies the two types of disease	56
Identifies the body's defenses against disease	47, 56
Identifies steps to manage stress	63
Learns how to make healthful choices to reduce the risk of disease	55–63
Describes the impact of tobacco use on personal health	57, 58
Discusses how to use medicines safely	61, 62
Distinguishes between prescription and over-the-counter medicines	61, 62
Distinguishes between medicine misuse and medicine abuse	61, 62
Explains how the use of illegal drugs can harm the body	61
Describes how alcohol affects health, abilities, and body functions	59, 60
Explains what blood alcohol level is and what it measures	59, 60
Nutrition	
Identifies the six basic nutrients	72
Describes the role of each type of nutrient in the body	72
Identifies the food groups used in the USDA Food Pyramid	67, 68, 69, 70, 71

Standards Correlation Chart continued

Standards	Pages
Explains how the Food Pyramid helps people obtain a balanced diet	67, 68, 69, 70, 71
Describes a healthful vegetarian diet	77
Recognizes that good health depends on making food choices that satisfy nutritional needs	76, 78
Explains how to use food labels to evaluate the nutrition of foods	75
Describes how to store and prepare food safely	78
Physical Education	
Understands the relationship between caloric intake and energy expenditure	73, 82
Identifies the four steps in goal setting	83
Practices goal setting for fitness	83, 86
Develops a personal exercise and fitness program	86
Knows the potential fitness benefits of various activities	82–88
Knows activities that promote a faster heart rate	82–87
Knows the proper warm-up, conditioning, and cool-down techniques and the reasons for them	88
Knows how proper stretching increases flexibility and knows why flexibility is important	88
Demonstrates smooth combinations of fundamental locomotor skills such as running and dodging or jumping	89–93
Knows various techniques for throwing or catching different objects	91–93
Knows basic skills and safety procedures to participate in outdoor sports	89–93
Knows how to demonstrate functional patterns of striking, dribbling, volleying, throwing, and catching in dynamic situations	91–93
Recognizes the proper techniques for performing an overhand throw	90, 91, 93
Throws a variety of objects demonstrating both distance and accuracy	90–93
Knows the reasons that appropriate practice improves performance	86, 91

Assessment

∞∞

🍎 **Darken the circle by the answer that best completes each sentence.**

1. The _____ is the first of five levels of organization in living things.
   - Ⓐ organ
   - Ⓑ tissue
   - Ⓒ system
   - Ⓓ cell

2. A group of organs working together makes up a _____.
   - Ⓐ body system
   - Ⓑ circulation chart
   - Ⓒ cell guide
   - Ⓓ muscle group

3. The _____ is the body part that identifies the messages of all the senses.
   - Ⓐ heart
   - Ⓑ brain
   - Ⓒ rib cage
   - Ⓓ spinal column

4. The sense of touch tells about how things feel, temperature, pressure, and _____.
   - Ⓐ pain
   - Ⓑ color
   - Ⓒ smell
   - Ⓓ noise

5. The _____ helps keep disease from entering the body.
   - Ⓐ heart
   - Ⓑ brain
   - Ⓒ skin
   - Ⓓ hair

6. The tongue can taste bitter, sweet, salty, and _____ flavors.
   - Ⓐ pepper
   - Ⓑ pickle
   - Ⓒ sour
   - Ⓓ chocolate

7. The skeleton _____ the body.
   - Ⓐ forms
   - Ⓑ supports
   - Ⓒ protects
   - Ⓓ all of the above

8. The _____ system moves materials to all parts of your body.
   - Ⓐ integumentary
   - Ⓑ circulatory
   - Ⓒ nervous
   - Ⓓ muscular

9. The excretory system removes _____ from the body.
   - Ⓐ blood
   - Ⓑ heat
   - Ⓒ waste
   - Ⓓ saliva

10. When you breathe in, your body takes in _____.
    - Ⓐ oxygen
    - Ⓑ carbon dioxide
    - Ⓒ salt
    - Ⓓ wastes

Go on to the next page.

∞∞

Assessment, p. 2

11. The endocrine system controls the _____ of the body.
   Ⓐ movement
   Ⓑ growth
   Ⓒ diseases
   Ⓓ senses

12. The _____ is the main organ of the circulatory system.
   Ⓐ heart
   Ⓑ lung
   Ⓒ liver
   Ⓓ brain

13. The _____ are the main organs of the respiratory system.
   Ⓐ intestines
   Ⓑ lungs
   Ⓒ kidneys
   Ⓓ ears

14. The _____ systems allow your body to move.
   Ⓐ endocrine and excretory
   Ⓑ integumentary and circulatory
   Ⓒ skeletal and muscular
   Ⓓ digestive and respiratory

15. Hormones are produced by _____.
   Ⓐ olfactories
   Ⓑ the diaphragm
   Ⓒ glands
   Ⓓ the excretory system

16. The word *reproduce* means _____.
   Ⓐ to make fewer
   Ⓑ to put out more apples and lettuce
   Ⓒ to make more
   Ⓓ old-fashioned

17. _____ is the passing of characteristics and traits from parents to children.
   Ⓐ Respiration
   Ⓑ Heredity
   Ⓒ Vibration
   Ⓓ Tissue

18. Drugs that speed up the functions of the body are called _____.
   Ⓐ stimulants
   Ⓑ amphetamines
   Ⓒ uppers
   Ⓓ all of the above

19. The _____ are the part of the body most affected by cigarette smoke.
   Ⓐ nerves
   Ⓑ muscles
   Ⓒ eyes
   Ⓓ lungs

20. Blood alcohol content (BAC) means the amount of alcohol per 100 units of _____.
   Ⓐ oxygen
   Ⓑ nerves
   Ⓒ blood
   Ⓓ saliva

Go on to the next page.

Name _____ Date _____

Assessment, p. 3

21. The Food Pyramid shows the food groups and the amount of each group you need to eat for a _____ diet.
    - (A) vegetarian
    - (B) balanced
    - (C) high-fat
    - (D) protein

22. Nutrients move into the bloodstream through the _____.
    - (A) small intestine
    - (B) stomach
    - (C) large intestine
    - (D) esophagus

23. The Food Pyramid shows that people need to eat fewer foods from the _____ group.
    - (A) oils
    - (B) milk
    - (C) grains
    - (D) vegetables

24. A _____ is the unit that measures the amount of energy in food.
    - (A) tablespoon
    - (B) decibel
    - (C) decameter
    - (D) calorie

25. Exercise makes your pulse rate _____.
    - (A) go down
    - (B) stay the same
    - (C) go up
    - (D) stop

26. Physical activity helps you to burn _____.
    - (A) water
    - (B) brain cells
    - (C) calories
    - (D) money

27. When you do physical activity, you should warm up and _____.
    - (A) chill out
    - (B) make toast
    - (C) quit
    - (D) cool down

28. Possible sources of stress are taking a test and _____.
    - (A) having an argument at home
    - (B) giving a speech
    - (C) being late to class
    - (D) all of the above

29. You dribble a soccer ball or a _____.
    - (A) basketball
    - (B) football
    - (C) baseball
    - (D) bowling ball

30. A ball spinning away from you is said to have _____.
    - (A) muscle tone
    - (B) backspin
    - (C) topspin
    - (D) fitness

Assessment
Health, Nutrition, and P.E. 5–6, SV 1419023608

Teacher Resource

Introduction

Health for children revolves around a basic understanding of the functions of the human body, healthy foods, plenty of exercise, and good hygiene. As children grow, they should recognize that they can make choices that will help them live healthy lives. They need to learn the connections between what they eat and the way they look and feel. They need to have the basic information that will help them to make good food choices. Children need to know that it is never too early to begin healthy habits in eating, exercise, and hygiene. The habits they form now will affect their lives for many years to come.

The Human Body

The cell is the first level of organization in the human body. Groups of cells that have the same structure are called tissues. An organ is a group of different kinds of tissues working together to do a job. A system is a group of organs working together to do a job.

Ten basic systems of the human body are covered in this unit.

Skeletal System: gives the body shape and support, protects inner organs

Muscular System: makes the body move

Circulatory System: transports materials to all parts of the body

Respiratory System: takes in oxygen and releases carbon dioxide

Digestive System: breaks down food into nutrients for cells to use

Excretory System: removes waste produced by cells

Nervous System: controls the body and helps it respond to the environment

Endocrine System: regulates growth and development, helps control some body functions

Integumentary System: skin, hair, and nails protect the body

Reproductive System: enables adults to produce offspring

Each of these systems is included in this unit. Some of them are mentioned briefly, while others are given more space. The amount of information necessary for the teacher to be successful in teaching these pages is complete on the pages themselves and in the answer key. Students are encouraged to use resource books to find answers to questions.

Bones, Joints, and Muscles

There are 206 bones in the human skeletal system that support, protect, and move the body. Bones also produce blood cells in their marrow. The marrow is in the hollowed center of the bone. In young people, all bones have red, blood-producing marrow. Older people have red marrow only in the flat bones, such as the ribs. The other bones contain yellow marrow that does not produce blood cells. Cartilage is a soft, rubbery substance that is found where some bones meet. It keeps the bones from rubbing together. You have cartilage at the end of your nose, too.

Bones join in three ways. A hinge joint allows the bone to move back and forth, as the knees and elbows do. A ball-and-socket joint, such as the shoulder joint, allows the body to move in many directions. A ball-shaped bone fits into the hollow of another bone. Pivot joints, like the one that joins the head to the spine, allow the bones to move around and back. Ligaments, strong bands of material that hold the bones in place, join bones at movable joints.

The human body has more than 600 muscles. Muscles enable us to move, keep some organs moving, and connect bones and skin together. Our muscles keep our blood moving, help us to digest, and keep our lungs expanding and contracting.

Some muscle movements are voluntary, and some are involuntary. Most voluntary muscles are connected to bones. (Tendons are tough cords that connect muscles to bones when they are not directly connected.) When you want to move your arm, you move your biceps and triceps. These muscles contract, and your arm moves. This movement is voluntary. A sheet of muscles under your lungs moves in and out without your conscious effort. These muscles make up the diaphragm. The movement of the diaphragm causes air to rush in and out of your lungs. This movement is involuntary. Some muscle movements are not wholly voluntary or involuntary. Can you control the blinking of your eyes? If you try to stop blinking altogether, you will see that you do not have complete control. Your eyes will blink.

When you decide you want to move, a message is sent to your brain. Your brain sends a message to the appropriate muscle to contract. The muscle shortens and becomes firm, and the movement occurs. When you want to stop the movement, your brain tells the muscle to relax. People who are physically fit have muscles that are never fully relaxed. They are always slightly flexed and firm. This is called muscle tone. To get muscle tone, large amounts of blood need to be supplied to the muscle cells. In order to get the blood to the muscle cells, a person must exercise. Muscles that do not get the necessary blood, or that do not get used enough, become weak and soft.

There are three kinds of muscle cells—smooth, cardiac, and skeletal. The smooth muscle cells are long and thin, and pointed at each end. They have one nucleus. An example of a smooth muscle is a stomach muscle. Cardiac muscles control the heart. The cardiac muscle cells branch out and weave together. They also have one nucleus. The skeletal muscle cells resemble straws and have many nuclei. The tongue and lips contain skeletal muscles.

Blood

Adults have about five liters of blood in their body. Children have about four liters of blood. Blood is a tissue that is more than half liquid. The liquid part of blood is called plasma. Plasma is mostly water. Red blood cells, white blood cells, and platelets float in the plasma. Red blood cells make up about half of the blood, and the white blood cells and platelets make up the rest. Red blood cells, which resemble tiny flattened balls, carry oxygen from the lungs to the body tissues, and take carbon dioxide from the tissues to the lungs. They are red because they contain a substance called hemoglobin. White blood cells, which are larger than red blood cells and irregular in shape, help fight off disease. After the protective covering cells of the skin, hair, and mucus, white blood cells are the body's second line of defense. If bacteria enter the body, white blood cells move toward them and "swallow" them. (The bacteria then leave the body in pus.) Platelets are important in the clotting of blood when the body is injured.

The Five Senses and the Nervous System

The human body collects information using the five senses—sight, smell, hearing, taste, and touch. The nervous system enables us to put all of our senses together so that messages are sent to the brain and we are able to act according to the information that the brain receives. The nervous system enables us to react. It controls all of the other systems in the body.

Health, Nutrition, and P.E. 5–6, SV 1419023608

The major organ of the nervous system is the brain. Another part of the nervous system is a system of nerves that carry information to the brain. The third part of the nervous system is the sense organs. The nose is the sense organ for the sense of smell. There are many nerve cells in the nose that take the information regarding odors to a main nerve called the olfactory nerve. The olfactory nerve carries the information to your brain. Your brain will then tell your body what to do with the information.

Hygiene

Keeping the body clean is an important part of staying healthy. Children need to know that when they wash, they are washing off viruses and bacteria, or germs, which can cause illness. Washing the hair and body regularly prevents bacteria from entering the skin through cuts and from getting into the mouth. Hands should always be washed after handling garbage or using the bathroom.

Germs can also come from other people. Children should be discouraged from sharing straws, cups, or other utensils. They should be reminded always to cover their mouths when they sneeze or cough, and to use tissues frequently. Children also need to be reminded not to share combs or hats.

Teeth

Regular brushing and flossing can help keep teeth healthy. Avoiding sweets will also help. Most children have all their baby teeth by the time they are two years old. When they are about seven, they begin to lose their baby teeth, and permanent teeth begin to appear. Although the baby teeth fall out, it is important to take good care of them and the gums that surround them.

Decay is caused by acids in the mouth that eat into the enamel. The acids are caused by bacteria that live on the food in your mouth. If you brush and floss regularly, the food is taken out of your mouth, and the bacteria cannot live there. When you brush, you remove the plaque from your teeth, as well. Plaque is the sticky yellow film that develops on your teeth from food, bacteria, and acid. Decay can cause a hole in the tooth called a cavity. It can also harm the gums and cause gum disease. Regular dental exams and X-rays will detect any decay that you may have missed.

Tobacco, Alcohol, and Drugs

Students in the upper elementary grades are often faced with difficult choices, such as whether to try smoking, drinking, or drugs. If students understand the health risks involved in smoking, drinking, and using drugs, they will be better prepared to make intelligent, informed choices. It is not enough to tell young people not to experiment with these things; they need to know the consequences.

Smoking

People have known for many years that smoking is unhealthy. Yet thousands of people continue to smoke, and young people still begin smoking, in spite of the dangers. Tobacco contains nicotine and tar, both harmful substances for the body. Nicotine raises blood pressure and increases the heart rate. A smoker's heart works harder than a nonsmoker's heart; it works harder than it should, increasing the risk for heart disease. When nicotine enters the circulatory system, the blood vessels narrow. The heart has to work harder to pump the blood through the body. Tar causes cancer in the lungs, throat, tongue, and lips. It destroys the tiny cilia in the trachea, causing emphysema. Both nicotine and tar damage the tiny air sacs in the lungs so that they can no longer exchange oxygen and carbon dioxide in an efficient manner. A look at the ragged, black lung of a smoker compared to the smooth, pink lung of a nonsmoker should be enough to give anyone second thoughts about smoking. Smokers have a much higher chance of getting heart, respiratory, and/or circulatory diseases than nonsmokers.

Health, Nutrition, and P.E. 5–6, SV 1419023608

Alcohol

The alcohol in beverages is called ethyl alcohol. It is the only alcohol that is not highly toxic, but it is still harmful. Alcohol affects a person's behavior, muscle control, senses, breathing, and heartbeat. The degree to which a person is affected depends on the amount of alcohol consumed and the body weight of the person.

Alcohol is a depressant—it lowers the action of the muscular and nervous systems, including the brain and spinal cord. Heavy drinking can destroy brain cells. Alcohol enters the blood system much faster than food. The amount of alcohol in a person's system can be determined by a breath test. In many places, someone with a blood alcohol level of .08 to .10 is considered legally intoxicated. Only a few drinks are needed to reach that level.

Drugs

Students should be aware of the differences between helpful and harmful drugs. The drugs that can be bought over the counter at the drugstore help us when used correctly. Drugs prescribed by doctors keep people healthy and alive. People who do not take these drugs as prescribed by their doctor are drug abusers. It is not safe to take any medication in any way other than the way it is prescribed or recommended. Barbiturates, often prescribed as sleeping pills, and amphetamines, prescribed as diet pills, are often misused. Amphetamines can speed up the body's systems, and barbiturates can slow them down. Combining these drugs with alcohol is particularly dangerous.

Other drugs are used that are not sold in stores or prescribed by doctors—these drugs are illegal. Marijuana is a well-known illegal drug. The chemicals in marijuana can stay in the brain for weeks and affect short-term memory. The smoke can harm the lungs. Sniffing fumes from hair sprays, paint thinner, or glue can cause dizziness and vomiting. The vapors use up oxygen in the blood and prevent the user from breathing.

Choices

Tobacco, alcohol, and drugs are all addictive. Addictions are not habits, but diseases. There are programs that can help both teens and adults to cope with their addictions. But the road to recovery can be long and painful; often, it is a lifelong struggle. Clearly, the best choice for students is the healthy choice—saying no to smoking, alcohol, and drugs from the start. It can be awkward and difficult for young people to take a stand and stay drug free. If they are given the information and understand the risks, they may gain the confidence necessary to make good decisions. Ultimately, they are the ones who must choose to take care of themselves.

Health, Nutrition, and P.E. 5–6, SV 1419023608

Bulletin Board: All Systems Go!

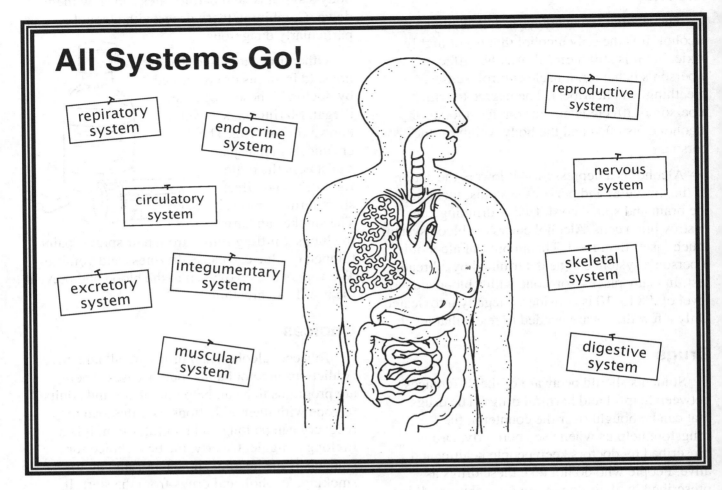

Materials

craft paper	markers	tape
note cards	scissors	stapler

Teacher Directions

1. Prepare a bulletin board with background paper of your choice. Add the title "All Systems Go!"
2. Trace a cutaway human torso as shown on this page. You can show only the upper torso.
3. Decide which of the body systems you want to illustrate in the torso cutaway. Some teachers may not want to show the reproductive or excretory systems.
4. Divide the class into groups, one group for each body system you want to illustrate in the torso.
5. Assign a body system to each group of students. The students should use a health textbook, an encyclopedia, or the Internet to do research on their body system.
6. Have the students draw the body parts associated with the body system. The students should write the name of the system on a note card.
7. Give each group time to place the body system in the cutaway torso and attach the note card. A line should be drawn from the note card to the main organs in that system.
8. If you like, you can have the group prepare an oral report to be given using the bulletin board as a visual aid.

Cells—The Body's Smallest Parts

Look at the period at the end of this sentence. You may be surprised to learn that your body is made of parts that are smaller than that period! Your body is made of **cells**. All living things are made of cells. Most cells are too small to see with your eyes alone. You have to use a tool called a microscope.

The cells of your body are like tiny factories. Each cell takes in food, and each cell gives off wastes. To live, a cell must do these jobs over and over. Cells can also grow and divide. When a cell divides, one cell becomes two cells. Then two cells become four cells, and so on. Dividing cells make you grow. Bone cells divide and make bones grow. Muscle cells divide and make muscles grow. Even after you stop growing, your cells keep dividing. You can see this with skin cells. Suppose you fall and cut the skin on your knee. Your skin cells divide and make more cells. In about a week, new cells have filled in the cut.

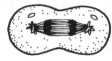

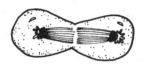

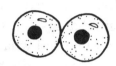

A Cell Dividing

Your body has millions and millions of cells. These cells have many different jobs. Bone cells do a special job, and blood cells do another job. But all the cells of your body work together. Together they do the job of living.

🍎 **Write *true* or *false*.**

_____ **1.** Cells are in all living things.

_____ **2.** You need a microscope to see some cells.

_____ **3.** You are made of one huge cell.

_____ **4.** Cells divide and make more cells.

_____ **5.** You grow because your cells divide.

_____ **6.** When you stop growing, your cells stop dividing.

🍎 **Write complete sentences to tell about the two jobs of a cell.**

7. _____

_____

_____

13
Unit 1: Health
Health, Nutrition, and P.E. 5–6, SV 1419023608

Name _____ Date _____

The Parts of a Cell

You know that cells are very small, but even tiny cells have different parts. Most cells have a membrane. The membrane is like your skin. When you sweat, wastes pass out of your skin. Wastes also pass out of the cell. They move out through the cell membrane. Food can move into the cell through the cell membrane.

The Cell and Its Parts

Cells are filled with **protoplasm**, which is a clear jelly. It holds many other small cell parts. Some of these parts store food and do other special jobs for the cell. Most cells have a **nucleus**. The nucleus is like a tiny brain that gives instructions to the cell. It tells a cell what kind it will be and what its job is in the body. The only cell in the body that does not have a nucleus is a red blood cell.

Some cells do special jobs. The way a cell looks is often a clue to the kind of work it does. Fat cells store large amounts of fat in the protoplasm. Nerve cells carry messages through the body. They have long parts, like telephone wires, that carry messages from one part of the body to another. Skin cells are flat and protect the parts of the body that they cover.

 Draw lines between the cell part and the job it does.

1. Protoplasm   tells the cell what its job is.

2. Nucleus   lets food and wastes in and out of the cell.

3. Membrane   holds small parts of the cell.

 Write a complete sentence to tell what nerve cells do.

4. _____

_____

_____

Health, Nutrition, and P.E. 5–6, SV 1419023608

Name _____ Date _____

Tissues

You know that cells are the smallest part of your body. You also know that different cells have different jobs. Cells do not work alone, however. Cells that look alike and that do the same job work together in a group. A group of cells doing the same job is called a **tissue**.

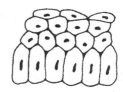

Skin Tissue

Muscle Tissue

Your body has four kinds of tissues. A group of skin cells doing the same job is called **skin tissue**. One kind of skin tissue covers your body. Another kind of skin tissue lines your mouth, stomach, and other body parts. Bundles of muscle cells form **muscle tissue**. Muscle tissue is made up of cells that contract when they receive signals from the brain. The contracting and relaxing of muscle tissue moves the skeleton. The signals that trigger the muscles travel through **nerve tissue**. The brain and spinal cord are made of nerve tissue. So are all the places where the senses begin. **Connective tissue** is found in bones, cartilage, and tendons. Blood is also a connective tissue.

🍎 **Choose words from the ( ) to complete the sentences.**

1. Cells _____ work alone.   (do, do not)

2. The smallest part of your body is a _____.   (cell, tissue)

3. A tissue is made up of _____.   (bones, cells)

4. Your body is covered by _____ tissue.   (skin, muscle)

🍎 **Write complete sentences to answer the questions.**

5. What is a tissue? _____

_____

6. What are the four kinds of body tissue? _____

_____

_____

_____

Organs

What is happening as you read this page? Your heart is pumping. You breathe in and out with your lungs. Your eyes see the words on the page, and your brain helps you understand the words. All these body parts are examples of organs. An **organ** is a group of different tissues working together to do a job.

Each organ in a person's body performs a special job that keeps the person alive. Your heart is made of connective tissue, nerve tissue, and muscle tissue. What is the job of your heart? Your skin has many different layers. Each layer has a different job. All the parts of your skin combine to form an organ. Your stomach is an organ that helps in the job of breaking down food.

 Write *true* or *false*.

_____ **1.** An organ is a group of different tissues working together.

_____ **2.** Your heart is a tissue.

_____ **3.** Your eyes are organs.

_____ **4.** A cell is larger than an organ.

_____ **5.** Your brain is one cell.

 Choose words from the ( ) to complete the sentences.

6. Cells work together in groups called _____. (organs, tissues)

7. A group of tissues working together is called _____. (an organ, a tissue)

8. Your lungs are examples of _____. (cells, organs)

Lungs

Heart

Stomach

Health, Nutrition, and P.E. 5–6, SV 1419023608

Name _____ Date _____

Systems Working Together

Do you remember how your body is organized? The smallest parts of your body are its cells. A group of cells doing the same job forms a tissue. A group of tissues working together forms an organ. Organs work in groups, too. A group of organs doing the same job is called a **system**. Your body is made up of many systems.

Systems in the body work together to get things done. The digestive system, the circulatory system, and the respiratory system work together to provide your body cells with food and oxygen they need to function. The digestive system turns the food you eat into nutrients that the body can use. At the same time, the respiratory system brings oxygen into the lungs. Oxygen passes from the lungs into the circulatory system, and nutrients pass from the small intestine into the circulatory system. In the circulatory system, the blood carries the oxygen and nutrients to all the cells of the body. The skeletal system and the muscular system move your body. The nervous system tells every part of the body what to do.

Remember:
- Cells are the basic units of all living things.
- Groups of cells with the same function are called tissues.
- Groups of tissues with the same function are called organs.
- Organs with related functions belong to a system.

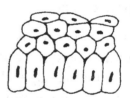

 Match the terms at the right with the definitions on the left. Write the letter of the term on the line by its definition.

_____ **1.** a body structure made of different kinds of tissues that work together to do a specific job

_____ **2.** groups of cells with the same structure and function

_____ **3.** the basic unit of structure and function of an organism

_____ **4.** fluid tissue that moves from place to place

_____ **5.** a group of organs that work together to do a job

A. cell

B. tissues

C. organ

D. system

E. blood

 Write complete sentences to answer the question.
The second paragraph above tells some ways the body systems work together. Can you think of another way that the systems of the body work together?

6. _____

_____

Name _____   Date _____

The Skeletal System

Your **skeleton** is made up of 206 bones of different shapes and sizes. There are tiny bones in your fingers and long bones in your arms and legs. Bones are made of connective tissue. All the bones are part of your **skeletal system**. The bones of the skeletal system work together with muscles to make your body move.

Your skeletal system has many functions. Its primary function is to support and protect the soft tissues and organs of your body. In addition to support and protection, your skeletal system helps you move. Bones, joints, and muscles work together to allow you to pedal your bicycle, type at a computer keyboard, kick a soccer ball, and climb the stairs, among many other movements.

Bones are also important because they produce **blood cells**. Red **marrow** produces red blood cells, some white blood cells, and cell fragments. Red marrow is found in the long bones of your body, which include the humerus and the femur. Red marrow is also in the ribs, the sternum, the vertebrae, and the pelvic bones.

Bones also act as storehouses for **minerals**. Calcium and phosphorus are two minerals stored in bones. Calcium makes your bones strong. It is also important in relaying messages through the nervous system and in helping muscles contract. Phosphorus helps regulate blood chemistry and also plays a part in muscle contraction and nerve activity.

 Answer these questions.

1. How many bones are in your skeleton? _____

_____

2. What is the primary function of your skeletal system? _____

_____

3. What three body parts allow you to move in many different ways? _____

_____

4. What does red marrow do and where is it found? _____

_____

5. What two minerals are stored in bones? _____

_____

Health, Nutrition, and P.E. 5–6, SV 1419023608

Name _____ Date _____

Joints

You would not be able to move your body without joints. A **joint** is a place where two bones come together. At every joint, bones are held together by strong connective tissues called **ligaments**. Together, joints and ligaments let bones move. There are three main kinds of movable joints in the body.

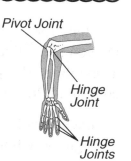

Pivot Joint

Hinge Joint

Hinge Joints

Hinge joints work like the hinge of a door. They can bend back and forth in only one direction. You have hinge joints in your elbows and knees. You also have hinge joints in your fingers and toes. These joints let you move the many small bones in your hands and feet.

Ball-and-Socket Joint

Your head is connected to your backbone by a **pivot joint**. A pivot joint can move around and back. This joint lets you twist your head around and look over your shoulder. You can also bend your head back or forward.

Remember that your elbow has a hinge joint, but it also has a pivot joint. This joint lets your arm twist so you can do things like turn a doorknob.

The joint that allows the most movement is a **ball-and-socket joint**. It can move in all directions. In a ball-and-socket joint, the end of one bone is shaped like a ball. It fits into a curved space at the end of the other bone. Your shoulders and hips have this kind of joint. A ball-and-socket joint can move in a complete circle. This lets you make the movements to throw a baseball or swim.

The parts of your **skull** also have joints, but the joints in the skull are immovable. They do not allow any movements.

🍎 **Darken the circle by the answer that best completes each sentence.**

1. Bones come together at _____.
   - Ⓐ ligaments
   - Ⓑ joints
   - Ⓒ elbows
   - Ⓓ tissues

2. Hinge joints bend _____.
   - Ⓐ in one direction
   - Ⓑ in many directions
   - Ⓒ all around
   - Ⓓ no directions

3. Bones are held together by _____.
   - Ⓐ tape
   - Ⓑ bone glue
   - Ⓒ ligaments
   - Ⓓ doorknobs

4. Your fingers contain _____.
   - Ⓐ hinge joints
   - Ⓑ ball-and-socket joints
   - Ⓒ pivot joints
   - Ⓓ immovable joints

Health, Nutrition, and P.E. 5–6, SV 1419023608

Parts of the Skeleton

Bend forward and run your fingers down the middle of your back. Do you feel a line of bones? Each of the small bones you feel is called a **vertebra**. Many vertebrae are stacked on top of each other. This column of 26 vertebrae forms the **backbone**, or **spine**.

Each vertebra has a hole in the middle. The **spinal cord** goes through these holes. It is part of your nervous system. The spinal cord connects your brain with other parts of your body. An injury to the spinal cord could prevent parts of the body from moving. The important job of the backbone is to protect the spinal cord.

Attached to the backbone are 12 pairs of bones. These bones, or ribs, curve around the body. They form a kind of cage. The **rib cage** protects the heart and lungs. Ten of the bone pairs are attached to the breastbone at the front of the cage.

Another group of bones protects your eyes and brain. These bones form the skull. It may feel like one large, round bone, but the skull is really made up of many bones. The bones of your face are also part of the skull.

Most of the skeleton is made of bone, but the skeleton also contains a softer material called **cartilage**. Cartilage is a connective tissue that can bend without breaking. Unborn babies first have skeletons of cartilage. Then the cartilage hardens and becomes bone before the baby is born. Some cartilage remains in the skeleton. It is found between bones as a kind of cushion. It can also be found in your ears and the tip of your nose.

Skull

Breastbone

Rib Cage

Backbone

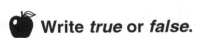 **Write *true* or *false*.**

_____ **1.** The backbone is made up of many vertebrae.

_____ **2.** The ribs protect the brain.

_____ **3.** Cartilage is softer than bone.

_____ **4.** The ribs are attached to the skull.

_____ **5.** Cartilage can be found in your nose and ears.

Skeleton Puzzle

There are 206 bones in your body. They are all different sizes and shapes. Together, they make up the skeletal system. The skeletal system has several important jobs. First, it supports the body. Bones also give you shape so you will have a form. Without the bones, you would not be able to stand. The skeleton also protects the soft parts of the body, like the brain and heart. Bones also work with the muscles to help you move.

 Work the crossword puzzle about the skeletal system.

Across

1. Bones and _____ work together to help you move.

3. The bones _____ the body to help you stand.

4. Bones _____ the soft body parts.

Down

2. All 206 bones make up the _____ system.

3. You have _____ and form because of bones.

Unit 1: Health
Health, Nutrition, and P.E. 5–6, SV 1419023608

The Muscular System

Your body has about 600 muscles. All these muscles working together form the **muscular system**. Working with the skeletal system, the muscular system produces movement in the body. Muscles cover the skeleton. They also line the walls of some organs, such as the heart and stomach.

Muscles are connected to bones by strong connective tissues called **tendons**. Tendons are like ligaments, but they do different jobs. Tendons connect muscles to bones. Ligaments connect bones to bones.

How do muscles move bones? A muscle attached to a bone **contracts**, or gets shorter, when it works. As it gets shorter, it pulls on the bone it is attached to. When a muscle stops working, it relaxes and goes back to its regular size. By changing their length, muscles move the bones they are attached to. Cardiac muscles move the blood through your body. Smooth muscles move food and wastes through your body.

Muscle tone is achieved through exercise. If a person has good muscle tone, the muscles do not completely relax. They are always slightly contracted. For you to have good muscle tone, plenty of blood needs to reach the muscle cells. This requires exercise.

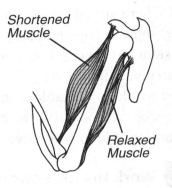

Shortened Muscle

Relaxed Muscle

Arm Bent

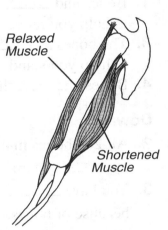

Relaxed Muscle

Shortened Muscle

Arm Straight

 Darken the circle by the answer that best completes each sentence.

1. There are about _____ muscles in the human body.

   Ⓐ 60   Ⓑ 600   Ⓒ 6,000   Ⓓ 13

2. Muscles are connected to bones with _____.

   Ⓐ tendons   Ⓑ tentacles   Ⓒ ligaments   Ⓓ skeletons

3. To have good muscle tone, you must _____.

   Ⓐ eat a lot   Ⓑ relax often   Ⓒ exercise   Ⓓ run 100 miles a day

4. Muscles _____ to move bones.

   Ⓐ contract   Ⓑ ligament   Ⓒ conclude   Ⓓ tone

Kinds of Muscles

Muscles can be voluntary or involuntary. **Voluntary muscles** are the ones that you can control. You can tell them when to move. Most voluntary muscles are attached to bones. **Involuntary muscles**, like those of the heart, move without your having to think about them. The muscles that control your eyelids may seem like voluntary muscles. You can blink your eyes when you want to. However, you cannot keep your eyes from blinking when they need to! You do not have complete control over them.

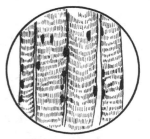
Skeletal Muscle

There are three kinds of muscle tissue in the muscular system. One kind is **skeletal muscle** tissue. Skeletal muscles move the bones of the skeleton. These muscles are long and shaped like cylinders (similar to straws). Unlike the other muscle cells, the skeletal muscles have many nuclei. The tongue and lips are skeletal muscles, as are the biceps and triceps in your arms. Most skeletal muscles are voluntary.

Cardiac Muscle

Cardiac muscle tissue is a second kind of muscle tissue. Cardiac muscles make up the heart. These muscles branch out and weave together. Their function is to pump blood. Some cardiac muscles work together to set the heartbeat rate. They ensure that all the cardiac muscles beat at the same time.

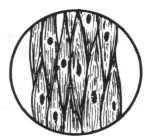
Smooth Muscle

The third kind is called **smooth muscle** tissue. The smooth muscles are long and thin and pointed at each end. Smooth muscles contract slowly and move substances through the organs they surround. These muscles run in bands around the walls of blood vessels and digestive organs. The stomach has smooth muscle cells. Smooth muscles also help move wastes through the large intestine.

 Choose words from the ( ) to complete the sentences.

1. The muscles you can control are called _____ muscles. (involuntary, weak, voluntary)

2. The heart is made of _____ muscles. (skeletal, cardiac, smooth)

3. The stomach is made of _____ muscles. (skeletal, cardiac, smooth)

4. The _____ muscles have many nuclei. (skeletal, cardiac, smooth)

Name _____   Date _____

Muscle Cells

 Complete these exercises.

A. Each of the following is a description of a type of muscle cell.
   Rewrite the description under the proper heading below.

Descriptions:
• Muscle cells that branch out and weave together. They make up the heart.
• Long, thin, and pointed cells
• Long, cylinder-shaped cells

1. Skeletal Muscle _____

   _____

2. Cardiac Muscle _____

   _____

3. Smooth Muscle _____

   _____

B. Draw a diagram that shows what muscle cells from each of the following
   body parts would look like. Use a health book if you need to.

4. Biceps   5. Heart   6. Stomach

Health, Nutrition, and P.E. 5–6, SV 1419023608

Flex Your Thinking Muscles

Read the following information. Then, using information from the paragraph or other sources, classify each muscle listed below as either *voluntary* or *involuntary*. Then, classify each muscle as *smooth*, *cardiac*, or *skeletal*. The first one has been done for you.

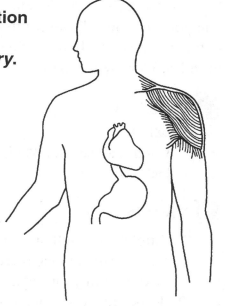

There are over 600 muscles in your body. Most of these are voluntary muscles. A voluntary muscle is a muscle over which you have control. When you want to pick up a pencil on your desk, you use voluntary muscles in your arm, hands, and fingers, and you pick up the pencil. Muscles that function without your having to think about them are involuntary muscles. For example, you don't have to think to keep your heart beating. Your body does it automatically.

1. heart muscle _____ involuntary, cardiac _____

2. finger muscles _____

3. stomach muscles _____

4. muscles in the eyes _____

5. intestinal muscles _____

6. triceps _____

7. muscles in the bladder _____

8. leg muscles _____

Health, Nutrition, and P.E. 5–6, SV 1419023608

Muscle Tone

How strong you are depends on your **muscle tone**. Good muscle tone means that your muscle cells are well-nourished. Exercising brings blood carrying food to the muscle cells. In this activity, you will measure the strength of some of your muscles. Work with a partner.

 Materials

- textbook
- watch with second hand
- desktop

 Do This

1. Stretch your left arm out on the desktop so the backs of your upper arm, elbow, lower arm, and hand are all touching the desktop. Ask your partner to put the textbook in your outstretched hand. Grasp the book firmly.
2. Raise the book toward your head. Count how many times you can touch the top of your head with the textbook in 30 seconds. Record your data.
3. Rest for 1 minute. Repeat with your right arm. Then, have your partner do the activity.

| Number of lifts | Left arm _____ | Right arm _____ |

Answer these questions.

1. Study your data. Which of your arms had the better muscle tone?

   _____

2. Make a hypothesis that explains any differences between the strength of

   your right and left arms. _____

   _____

3. What exercises could you do to strengthen the muscles of your arms?

   _____

4. Would it be easier to improve muscle tone for voluntary muscles or involuntary

   muscles? Explain. _____

   _____

Health, Nutrition, and P.E. 5–6, SV 1419023608

Name _____ Date _____

The Circulatory System

The **circulatory system** transports oxygen, nutrients, and wastes through the body in the blood. How do you think blood gets from one part of the body to another?

Blood is one part of the circulatory system. The other two parts of the system are the heart and the blood vessels. All the parts of the circulatory system have important jobs. The heart is the pump that keeps blood moving. The blood vessels are the paths the blood takes. The vessels can be large or small.

Blood moves through the circulatory system. It carries food and oxygen to the body cells. Inside the cells, food and oxygen mix to release the energy needed for life. As they make energy, cells also make wastes. One of these wastes is a gas called **carbon dioxide**. The blood carries carbon dioxide away from the cells. If wastes were not removed, the body would be poisoned.

The circulatory system helps protect the body from disease. Certain cells and chemicals can fight the germs that cause disease. The blood carries these germ fighters to the part of the body where they are needed.

When you exercise, you may begin to feel warm. Your circulatory system helps to keep you cool. Blood takes heat away from your organs. It carries the heat to your skin. The heat can then leave your body through your skin.

The Circulatory System

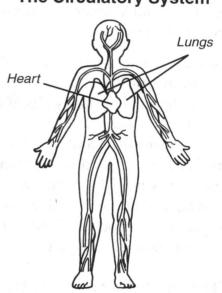

Lungs

Heart

 Write words from the box to complete each sentence.

| blood   carbon dioxide   cell   heart   oxygen |

1. The circulatory system delivers food and _____ to the cells.

2. The _____ is the pump that keeps the blood moving.

3. The blood takes the gas _____ away from the cells.

4. Blood must reach each _____ in every part of the body.

5. Germ fighters are carried by the _____.

Unit 1: Health
Health, Nutrition, and P.E. 5–6, SV 1419023608

Blood and Blood Vessels

When you cut yourself, you see the bright red liquid called blood. Blood is made of both liquids and solids. About half of blood is liquid. The liquid part of blood, called **plasma**, is mostly water. It also contains dissolved nutrients and waste products, such as carbon dioxide. The solid part of blood includes **red blood cells** and **white blood cells**. Red blood cells absorb oxygen from air in the lungs and transport it to every cell in the body. White blood cells help the body fight infection. They attack and destroy viruses and bacteria that enter the body. Blood also contains **platelets**—tiny pieces of blood cells inside membranes. Platelets cause blood to clot when a **blood vessel** is cut. They also help repair damage to blood vessels.

Think of the circulatory system as a delivery service. Then you can think of the blood vessels as roads. Blood vessels come in different sizes. Some are large. They are like highways. Others are smaller. They are like wide and narrow streets. The largest blood vessels are called **arteries**. Arteries carry blood away from the heart. The blood they carry is rich in oxygen.

Arteries divide into smaller and smaller blood vessels. The smallest blood vessels are called **capillaries**. The blood in the capillaries carries food and oxygen. These materials pass through the thin walls of the capillaries into the body cells. The body cells take the food and oxygen they need. Then the blood moves back into the capillaries. From the capillaries, the blood moves into **veins**. Veins are larger than capillaries but smaller than arteries. They bring blood that has lost its food and oxygen back to the heart. In the heart and lungs, the blood gets a new supply of food and oxygen. It also loses the wastes it is carrying.

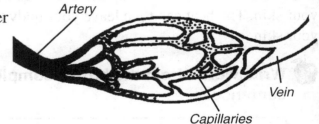

Artery

Vein

Capillaries

 Write complete sentences to answer the questions.

1. Which type of blood vessel carries blood away from the heart?

_____

2. Which type of blood vessel returns blood to the heart?

_____

3. Which blood vessels do body cells get food and oxygen from?

_____

_____

Health, Nutrition, and P.E. 5–6, SV 1419023608

The Heart

The **heart** is an organ made of muscle tissue. The heart is one of the most important organs in your body. It is not much larger than a fist. Your heart is really a double pump. The two pumps are separated by a wall of tissue that runs down the middle of the heart. The right side pumps blood to the lungs. The left side pumps blood to other parts of the body. Valves keep blood flowing in only one direction. Each side of the heart is divided into two **chambers**. The upper chamber is called an **atrium**, and the lower chamber is called a **ventricle**.

Blood that needs oxygen flows into the right atrium. From the right atrium, blood passes to the right ventricle. The blood is then pumped to the lungs. In the lungs, the blood cells get the oxygen they need. They also get rid of carbon dioxide. As red blood cells take in oxygen and give up carbon dioxide, they change in color from dark red to bright red.

The blood then leaves the lungs and passes through the heart again—this time to the left atrium, then the left ventricle. The heart pumps it through the large arteries into the smaller arteries and capillaries throughout the body. There, oxygen and nutrients are distributed to all the other cells, and wastes are picked up. The blood becomes dark red again. Then the blood returns through a vein to the heart—the right atrium—to begin its trip once more.

Each time the heart "beats," it pushes blood in two directions at once. Some of the blood goes to the lungs, and some of the blood goes to the rest of the body. If you have ever heard a heartbeat, you know that it makes a "puh-pum" type of sound. The "puh" sound is made when the valves of the heart close and push the blood one way, and the "pum" is the sound of different valves pushing the blood the other way. Each beat of the heart is a double pump. The heart pushes your blood through your body about once every minute.

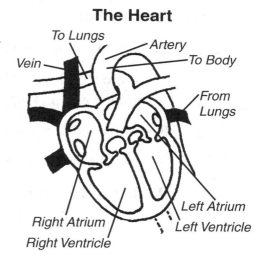

The Heart

To Lungs

Artery

Vein

To Body

From Lungs

Right Atrium

Right Ventricle

Left Atrium

Left Ventricle

When you are exercising, your body needs more food and oxygen than normal, so your heart beats faster. When you are sleeping, your heart beats more slowly, but it does not stop beating. It began to beat before you were born, and it keeps on beating throughout your whole life.

 Write complete sentences to answer the question.

Why do you think a healthy heart is important?

_____

_____

Name _____ Date _____

The Flow of Blood

The diagram below shows the circulatory system of the human body. Label the numbered parts of the circulatory system. Use a health book if you need to.

 Trace the pathway through which blood flows through the system so that it makes a complete loop, beginning and ending at number 1. Use a colored pencil.

1. _____

2. _____

3. _____

4. _____

5. _____

 Match each numbered section of the diagram with its description below. Write the number on the line in front of the description.

_____ **6.** smallest of all blood vessels

_____ **7.** where red blood cells drop off carbon dioxide and pick up oxygen

_____ **8.** carries blood away from the heart

_____ **9.** pumps blood throughout the body

_____ **10.** carries blood to the heart

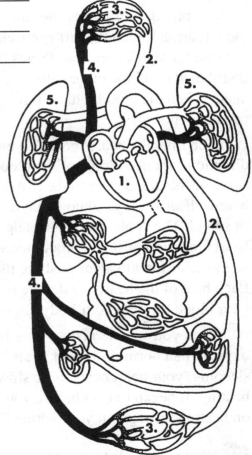

Health, Nutrition, and P.E. 5–6, SV 1419023608

Name _____ Date _____

The Respiratory System

All your body cells need oxygen. Without oxygen, your body cells cannot produce energy. The organs of your **respiratory system** bring oxygen into your body for your cells. They also get rid of the wastes given off by the cells. The main organs of the respiratory system are the **lungs**. How does the respiratory system work?

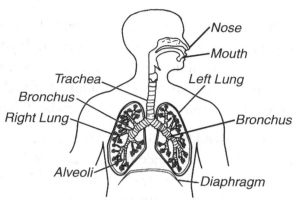

The Respiratory System

To breathe, you need the help of your muscular system. A large muscle called the **diaphragm** controls your lungs. When the diaphragm moves down, air is pulled into the lungs. When the diaphragm moves up, air is forced out of the lungs.

When you breathe in, or **inhale**, several liters of air are pulled into your body. The air is filtered by tiny hairs in your nose and warmed by capillaries that line the nasal passages. Warm, clean air then travels down your **trachea**, or windpipe.

In your chest, the trachea branches into two tubes called **bronchi**. Each tube, called a **bronchus**, leads into a lung. In the lungs, the bronchi divide into smaller and smaller tubes. At the end of the smallest tubes are tiny air sacs called **alveoli**. The walls of the alveoli are only one cell thick and are surrounded by capillaries. The capillaries surrounding the alveoli get blood from the **pulmonary arteries** coming from the heart. This blood contains a lot of carbon dioxide. Carbon dioxide is a waste produced by the process that releases energy in cells. Carbon dioxide diffuses through the thin walls of the alveoli and into air that will be **exhaled**, or breathed out.

At the same time, oxygen from inhaled air **diffuses** through the alveoli and into red blood cells in the capillaries. The oxygen-rich blood then flows from the capillaries into the **pulmonary veins** and back to the heart. From the heart, the oxygen-rich blood is pumped to other parts of the body.

Darken the circle by the answer that best completes each sentence.

1. The body needs oxygen to make _____.
   Ⓐ food   Ⓑ energy   Ⓒ blood   Ⓓ bones

2. The main organs of the respiratory system are the _____.
   Ⓐ air sacs   Ⓑ bronchi   Ⓒ lungs   Ⓓ diffuses

3. The lungs are controlled by the _____.
   Ⓐ windpipe   Ⓑ air sacs   Ⓒ nose hairs   Ⓓ diaphragm

4. After the nose, the air enters the _____.
   Ⓐ trachea   Ⓑ diaphragm   Ⓒ alveoli   Ⓓ blood

Health, Nutrition, and P.E. 5–6, SV 1419023608

Respiratory Puzzle

The respiratory system is responsible for the exchange of gases in the cells of the body. When you inhale, air passes through your nose, down your windpipe, and into two tubes called **bronchial tubes**. These tubes lead into your lungs. The tubes branch many times, like a tree, so that your lungs are filled with tiny tubes. The smallest tubes can only be seen with a microscope. At the ends of these tubes are air sacs.

Air is moved from the air sacs into the cells of the body by **diffusion**. This is the movement of a substance from an area with a lot of that substance to an area with less of that substance. When the oxygen-poor cells arrive in the lungs from the heart, the oxygen moves into the cells. The carbon dioxide, on the other hand, is more concentrated in the cells, so it moves out of the cells and into the air sacs. When you exhale, the carbon dioxide leaves your body by the same path by which the oxygen entered.

Breathing is only a partly voluntary movement. Part of the reason that you breathe is involuntary. It is caused by the movement of muscles called the **diaphragm**. This is a sheet of muscles beneath your lungs. When the diaphragm moves downward, it increases the space around the lungs, causing air to rush into your lungs. When the diaphragm moves up, it decreases the space around your lungs, and the air rushes out.

Do this crossword puzzle about the respiratory system.

Across
4. the system that brings oxygen to cells
6. the organ in which the oxygen-carbon dioxide exchange takes place
7. where oxygen goes when it leaves your nose
8. the outside organ that helps you breathe

Down
1. a sheet of muscles below your lungs
2. the tubes that lead into your lung
3. the way oxygen gets into cells
5. microscopic pocket of air in the lungs

32

Name _____ Date _____

Respiration Rates

In and out. In and out. Without even having to think about it, you constantly breathe—while you're reading this, while you eat a snack, even while you sleep. With each breath, your body gets the oxygen it needs and gives off carbon dioxide. Find out the number of times you breathe during the day.

 Materials

stopwatch, watch, or clock with second hand
calculator

 Do This

1. Your partner will tell you when to start—and 60 seconds later will tell you when to stop.
2. Sit very still. When your partner says "go," start counting your breaths. Remember, breathing in once and then breathing out counts as one breath.
3. Write your number of breaths in the space marked 1 minute in the table below.
4. Finish filling in the table below. To find out your number of breaths in an hour, multiply the number of breaths in 1 minute by 60. To find out how often you breathe in a day, multiply the number of breaths in an hour by 24. Multiply that number by 365 to find the number of breaths in a year.

Number of Breaths			
1 minute	1 hour	1 day	1 year

 Answer these questions.

1. Do you think your breathing rate, or how fast you breathe, can change? Explain your response.

_____

2. Test your response to the question above. Run in place for 30 seconds. Then repeat steps 1–3. Describe what happens.

_____

_____

Health, Nutrition, and P.E. 5–6, SV 1419023608

Name _____ Date _____

Does Holding Your Breath Change the Amounts of Oxygen and Carbon Dioxide You Exhale?

Materials

1-qt glass jar	clear plastic box
water	flexible drinking straw
cardboard	clock or watch with second hand
candle in candlestick	

Procedure

1. Have an adult light a candle. Place a jar over it. Record the time it takes the candle to go out.
2. Pour 6 to 8 cm of water into the plastic box.
3. Fill the jar with water. Cover the jar with cardboard.
4. Turn the jar over in the water of the plastic box. Remove the cardboard without letting air into the jar.
5. Bend the end of a straw. Put it under the rim of the jar.
6. Exhale through the straw, forcing the water out until there is no water left in the jar.
7. Have the adult light the candle again. Quickly cover the candle with the jar. Record how much time it takes for the candle to go out.
8. Repeat steps 2 through 7. This time, hold your breath for 10 seconds before exhaling.
9. Repeat steps 2 through 7 two more times. Each time, hold your breath 10 seconds longer than the time before.

Drawing Conclusions

1. Why did the candle go out? _____

2. How did the length of time the candle burned compare with the length of time you

   held your breath? _____

3. How does holding your breath change the amount of carbon dioxide you exhale?

   Explain. _____

   _____

   _____

34

Name _____ Date _____

The Digestive System

How does the body take what it needs from food? The body gets its raw materials from food by the process of digestion. **Digestion** is the breaking down of food into nutrients.

Your **digestive system** provides the nutrients your cells need to produce energy. To provide nutrients, the digestive system performs two functions. The first is to break food into nutrients. The second is to get the nutrients into the blood. Then the circulatory system transports them to your cells. Body cells use the nutrients to produce energy. The part of the food that the body cannot use is removed from the body. How does food travel through your body?

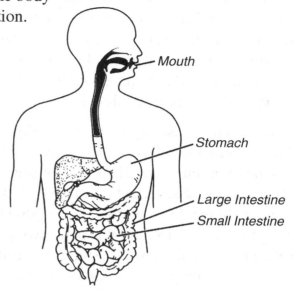

The Digestive System

Your digestive system is like a long tube. As food moves through the tube, it is changed by different organs. First, some organs grind up the food. Then, others change it by mixing it with chemicals. Next, other organs move the nutrients from the food into the blood. Finally, the unused part of the food is sent out of the body. The main organs of the digestive system are the **mouth**, the **stomach**, the **small intestine**, and the **large intestine**.

Food enters your body through your mouth. As your teeth grind up the food, it mixes with a liquid called **saliva**. Saliva contains a chemical that can change starch into sugar. Once the starch in your food has become sugar, it can pass into the blood. Then the body can use the sugar to make energy. When food leaves your mouth, it is still not completely digested. More starch needs to be changed into sugar. Proteins and fats have to be broken down. Digestion continues in the stomach.

Answer these questions.

1. What are the two functions of the digestive system?

_____

2. What are the four main organs of the digestive system?

_____

3. What is saliva?

_____

Digestion Continues

When you swallow, food passes through the **esophagus**, a long tube that leads to the stomach. **Gastric juice**, produced by the stomach, contains acid and chemicals that break down proteins. Stomach muscles act like a blender to mix the food. By the time the food leaves the stomach, it has become a liquid.

Next is the most important step of digestion. The partly digested food moves from the stomach into the small intestine. The small intestine is like a hose. If it were stretched out straight, it would be about 20 feet long. As food moves slowly along this "hose," its nutrients pass through the walls of the small intestine. Nutrients diffuse through the **villi**, projections sticking out of the walls of the small intestine, into the blood. Then the blood carries the nutrients to every cell in the body.

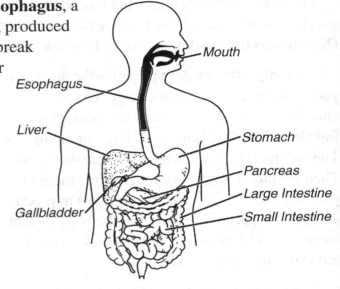

The Digestive System

The process of digestion is helped by other organs. The **liver** and the **gallbladder** pump chemicals into the small intestine. These chemicals help break down fats. The **pancreas** pumps in other chemicals. These chemicals break down fats as well as proteins and starches. When too much sugar is produced during digestion, the body has to store it. This is another job of the liver. It stores sugar that the body does not need.

Eventually, the food that is left passes out of the small intestine. From the small intestine, undigested food passes into the large intestine. There, water and minerals diffuse into the blood, and wastes are removed from the body.

🍎 **Darken the circle by the answer that best completes the sentence.**

1. Food travels from the mouth to the stomach through the _____.
   Ⓐ small intestine   Ⓑ large intestine   Ⓒ esophagus   Ⓓ gallbladder

2. The stomach produces _____ to break down proteins.
   Ⓐ orange juice   Ⓑ gastric juice   Ⓒ pancreas   Ⓓ sugar

3. In the small intestine, nutrients pass through _____ into the blood.
   Ⓐ blood gates   Ⓑ gastric juice   Ⓒ hoses   Ⓓ villi

4. The _____ stores sugar the body does not need.
   Ⓐ liver   Ⓑ stomach   Ⓒ pancreas   Ⓓ gallbladder

Name _____ Date _____

Saliva

∞∞

The digestion of food begins in your mouth. Your saliva contains an enzyme that breaks down starches into sugars. You can show that the digestion of starches begins in your mouth.

 Materials

plain, unsalted soda cracker
variety of foods such as bread, unsweetened cereal, celery

 Answer these questions.

1. A cracker contains starch. Take a bite of the cracker. How does it taste?

_____

2. Continue to chew the cracker for one minute.

How does it taste? _____

Why does it taste this way? _____

_____

_____

3. Now test some other foods. How can you find out if they contain starch?

_____

_____

4. Record your results in the chart below. Compare your results with those of your classmates.

Types of Food	Starch/No Starch
cracker	starch

∞∞

Health, Nutrition, and P.E. 5–6, SV 1419023608

The Excretory System

Once food leaves the small intestine, most of its usable parts have been removed. Only waste products and extra water are left. One job of the **excretory system** is to remove solid waste from the body.

The undigested food moves from the small intestine into the large intestine. Some water is removed for use by the body. The solid waste is pushed through the large intestine by muscles. In the large intestine, tiny organisms called **bacteria** begin to feed on the waste. Bacteria break down the waste.

Finally, the waste reaches the end of the large intestine. It passes through the last part of the digestive system. This is known as the **rectum**. Muscles in the rectum push waste out of the body.

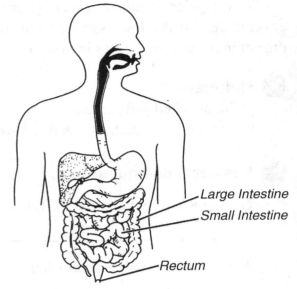

Large Intestine
Small Intestine

Rectum

The excretory system removes solid waste.

🍎 **Choose words from the ( ) to complete the sentences.**

1. After food leaves the small intestine, only _____ and water are left. (nutrients, waste)

2. The _____ is the last part of the digestive system. (rectum, small intestine)

3. In the large intestine, organisms called _____ feed on waste. (bacteria, nutrients)

🍎 **Write *true* or *false* for each statement.**

_____ 4. Muscles in the rectum push waste out of the body.

_____ 5. In the large intestine, some of the water is removed from food for use by the body.

Liquid Waste

The circulatory system supplies food and oxygen to the body's cells. It carries away waste products from the production of energy. The wastes must then be removed from the blood. The second function of the excretory system is to remove these liquid wastes.

Cell wastes include carbon dioxide and **ammonia**. As you have learned, the respiratory system gets rid of carbon dioxide. Ammonia is carried by the blood to the liver, where it is changed to **urea**. From the liver, urea is carried by the blood to the **kidneys**. These organs are located behind the liver and stomach. The kidneys are two bean-shaped organs about the size of your fist. The kidneys act as filters. As blood passes through them, the kidneys filter out water, salts, and harmful chemicals. The liquid that is produced is called **urine**.

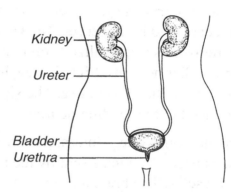

The excretory system removes liquid waste.

Urine, which is urea and water, flows from the kidneys through tubes called **ureters**. The ureters empty into a muscular organ called the **bladder**. When your bladder is full, you feel the need to empty it. Urine leaves the body through a channel called the **urethra**.

🍎 **Darken the circle by the answer that best completes each sentence.**

1. Cell wastes include carbon dioxide and _____.
   Ⓐ blood   Ⓑ ammonia   Ⓒ kidneys   Ⓓ water

2. The liver changes ammonia into _____.
   Ⓐ blood   Ⓑ water   Ⓒ urea   Ⓓ urine

3. Blood carries urea from the liver to the _____.
   Ⓐ bladder   Ⓑ urethra   Ⓒ bladder   Ⓓ kidneys

4. The kidneys filter the blood and produce a liquid called _____.
   Ⓐ urine   Ⓑ urea   Ⓒ ureter   Ⓓ urethra

🍎 **Write complete sentences to answer the question.**

5. What do you think would happen if wastes were not removed from the body?

_____

_____

_____

Health, Nutrition, and P.E. 5–6, SV 1419023608

The Nervous System

Your **nervous system** allows you to experience things and to react to your environment. It connects all the tissues and organs of your body to your **brain**. The nervous system consists of two parts—the central nervous system and the peripheral nervous system. The **central nervous system** is made up of the brain and the spinal cord. The **spinal cord** is a bundle of nerves, about as thick as a pencil. It runs from the base of the brain to the hips.

The **peripheral nervous system** consists of **sensory organs**, such as the eyes and ears, and body nerves. **Nerves** are bundles of nerve cells, or neurons. A **neuron** is a specialized cell that can receive signals and transmit them to other neurons. Signals traveling along nerves jump the gap between neurons. This gap is called a **synapse**. The signal is carried across the synapse by chemicals produced in the sending neuron.

The central nervous system interprets signals it receives from nerves and determines what response is needed. Signals sent by the brain travel through nerves and direct all of the body's muscles. The brain also controls the body's automatic functions, such as respiration, circulation, and digestion.

Some muscle actions are automatic responses to situations. These are called **reflexes**. For example, when a pain signal from a skin receptor reaches the spinal cord, the nerve carrying the signal transmits it directly to a nerve that controls muscles, as well as to a nerve traveling to the brain. The reflex action of the muscles to avoid the source of pain happens before the signal reaches the brain. In other words, you react to pain before you even feel pain.

Write complete sentences to answer the questions.

1. How are the central nervous system and the peripheral nervous system different?

   _____

   _____

   _____

2. What is a neuron? _____

   _____

   _____

3. What is a reflex? _____

   _____

Your Senses

The human body collects information using the five senses—sight, smell, hearing, taste, and touch. The nervous system helps your body respond to the environment. The brain is the main organ of the nervous system. The different sensory organs send messages through the nerves to the brain. The brain sorts out the messages to tell the body how to react.

Sensory organs contain neurons called **receptors**. Receptors are nerve cells that detect conditions in the body's environment. Receptors in the ears detect sound waves. Those in the skin detect heat and cold, pressure, touch, and pain. Receptors in the eyes detect light and color. Those in the mouth and nose detect tastes and smells. Each receptor sends a signal through nerves to the central nervous system.

The nose is the sensory organ for the sense of smell. As you breathe in, you take in tiny particles of all the things around you. The sensory nerves in the nose respond to these particles. The nerve cells in the nose send the information about odors to the **olfactory nerve**. This nerve is the main nerve for the sense of smell. The olfactory nerve carries the information to the brain. The brain will then give out information about what the smell is. The human brain can sense 50 different smells.

Darken the circle by the answer that best completes each sentence.

1. The five senses are sight, touch, smell, hearing, and _____.
   - Ⓐ taste
   - Ⓑ neurons
   - Ⓒ sleep
   - Ⓓ emotions

2. The _____ is the main organ of the nervous system.
   - Ⓐ nose
   - Ⓑ big toe
   - Ⓒ receptor
   - Ⓓ brain

3. _____ are nerve cells that detect conditions around your body.
   - Ⓐ Synapses
   - Ⓑ Receptors
   - Ⓒ Reflexes
   - Ⓓ Olfactories

4. The main nerve for the sense of smell is the _____.
   - Ⓐ brain
   - Ⓑ optic nerve
   - Ⓒ olfactory nerve
   - Ⓓ nose nerve

The Eye and Sight

Your eyes are sensory organs. Remember that sensory organs send different kinds of messages to the brain and the spinal cord. Your eyes send pictures of the world to your brain.

The colored part of your eye is called the **iris**. Look at the drawing of the eye and its parts. The opening at the center of the iris is the **pupil**. If there isn't much light, the pupil opens to let in more light. This makes it easier for you to see in dim light. In bright light, the pupil gets smaller. This protects your eye from too much light.

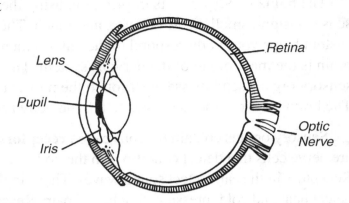

The **lens** of the eye can focus light to make sharp pictures. It focuses light onto the **retina**. The retina is a layer of tissue at the back of the eyeball. Sensory nerves cover the back of the eyeball. These sensory nerves send pictures to the **optic nerve**. The optic nerve sends the pictures to the brain. The brain understands what you see.

Your eyes are protected in many ways. The cheek and forehead bones can protect your eyes from injury. Eyelashes catch dirt and dust before they can get into your eyes. By blinking, your eyelids spread tears over your eyes. Tears help keep your eyes moist and clean. Remember that blinking is a reflex action.

You can help take care of your eyes. Do not rub them. You may be rubbing dirt into your eyes. Keep sharp objects away from your eyes. Wear glasses if you need them. See an eye doctor once a year to have your eyes checked.

Write *true* or *false* for each statement.

_____ 1. Your eyes can send messages to the brain.

_____ 2. If there is too much light, your iris gets larger.

_____ 3. The colored part of the eye is called the pupil.

_____ 4. The lens of the eye can focus light to make pictures.

_____ 5. Eyelashes help protect the eyes.

Health, Nutrition, and P.E. 5–6, SV 1419023608

Your Sense of Hearing

 The pictures show how you hear a dog when it barks. The sentences tell about the pictures. The sentences are not in the correct order. Write numbers to show the correct order of the sentences.

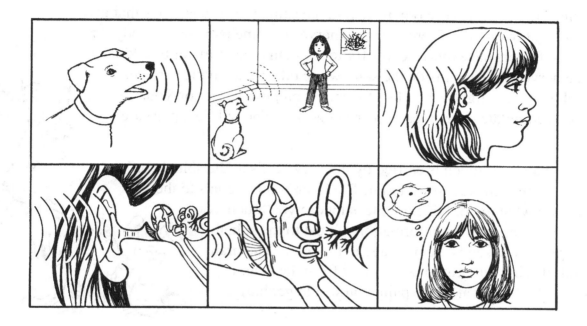

_____ The vibrating vocal cords bump the air molecules. These molecules start to vibrate. Sound waves form. They travel from the dog.

_____ The sound waves push against the eardrum and make it vibrate. The vibrating eardrum passes along the vibrations to three tiny bones, a liquid, and thousands of nerve endings.

_____ The dog barks. Its breath passes out of its throat and makes its vocal cords vibrate.

_____ The outer ear collects the sound waves. It brings them into the narrow canal inside the ear.

_____ Messages about the vibrations are sent along a large nerve to your brain. You recognize the sound as barking.

_____ Sound waves from the dog's vocal cords reach your ears.

Health, Nutrition, and P.E. 5–6, SV 1419023608

Name _____ Date _____

Your Sense of Touch

The sense of touch tells us when our body has made contact with another object. The sense of touch can give us information about the things we touch, and it tells us about temperature, pain, and pressure.

The skin is the largest sense organ. Within the skin are nerve endings that give us information about touch. There are more nerves in some parts of the body than in others. The fingers have more nerves for touch than other parts of the skin. Also, some nerves are deep inside the skin, while others are on the surface. If you touch your skin lightly, you feel touch. If you push harder on your skin, you will stimulate the nerves deeper in the skin. You will feel pressure and then pain.

The information of touch is carried by the nerve cells to the spinal cord. Then the message is moved to the brain. The brain sends signals to the body that tell it what to do. For example, suppose you touch a hot pan. Sensory nerves send the information of heat to the spinal cord. The spinal cord sends the message to the brain. The brain tells the muscles in your arm to move away from the heat. If you could not feel the heat or the pain, you would get hurt very easily.

Answer these questions.

1. What four things do the nerve endings in the skin react to?

   _____

   _____

2. Why do you think there are more nerve endings in the fingers than in other parts of the skin?

   _____

   _____

3. What would happen to someone touching a hot pan if that person did not have a sense of touch?

   _____

   _____

Health, Nutrition, and P.E. 5–6, SV 1419023608

Name _____ Date _____

Your Sense of Taste

Inside your mouth, there are many sensory nerves. These nerves bring messages to your brain about tastes. Special nerves are on the tongue. The nerves end in cells called **taste buds**. Taste buds can sense four flavors: sweet, sour, salty, and bitter. The buds send signals along the nerves to the brain, and the brain tells what flavors are in your mouth. Not all taste buds sense the same flavor. Look at the drawing of the tongue. Where are the taste buds for salty foods?

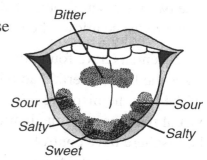

The Tongue

Do you remember the last time you had a cold? How did your favorite food taste? It probably didn't have much taste at all. That is because your sense of smell and sense of taste work together. When you can't smell food, it may be hard to taste it.

Sometimes taste and smell can give you important information. Foods that have a bad smell may be spoiled. They may not be safe to eat. Some things that taste bitter may be **poisonous**.

 Look at the words in the box. Write them in the chart under *Taste Order* **to show in what order they taste food. Then write the letters of each word on the lines in the column** *Code Words.* **Leave a blank line between the words. (Hint: Some words may have more lines than you need.)**

brain	taste buds	taste nerves

Taste Order	Code Words
1.	___ ___ ___ ___ ___ ___ ___ ___ ___ ___ ___ ___ 1 2 3 4 5 6 7 8 9 10 11 12
2.	___ ___ ___ ___ ___ ___ ___ ___ ___ ___ ___ ___ 13 14 15 16 17 18 19 20 21 22 23 24
3.	___ ___ ___ ___ ___ ___ ___ ___ ___ ___ ___ ___ 25 26 27 28 29 30 31 32 33 34 35 36

4. A secret code word contains these coded letters: 28, 5, 25, 4, 13, 21. Unscramble them

for the secret word: _____

Unit 1: Health
Health, Nutrition, and P.E. 5–6, SV 1419023608

Name _____   Date _____

Your Brain

Your brain is divided into two halves, or **hemispheres**. The two halves are connected by a band of tissue. This band of nerve tissue allows the two hemispheres to work together.

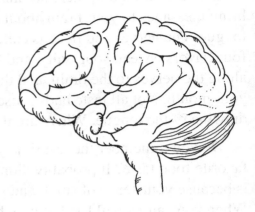

Scientists have found that one side of the brain sometimes takes the lead in certain activities. For example, certain areas of the right hemisphere have control over activities involving visual patterns and imagination. Certain areas of the left hemisphere have control over activities that involve words, numbers, facts, and figures.

Many people say that artists are "right-brained" and that math teachers are "left-brained." These labels are popular, but they can be misleading. One hemisphere of the brain may lead in certain activities, but both sides are always working together to perform tasks.

 Use the information above to complete the diagram.

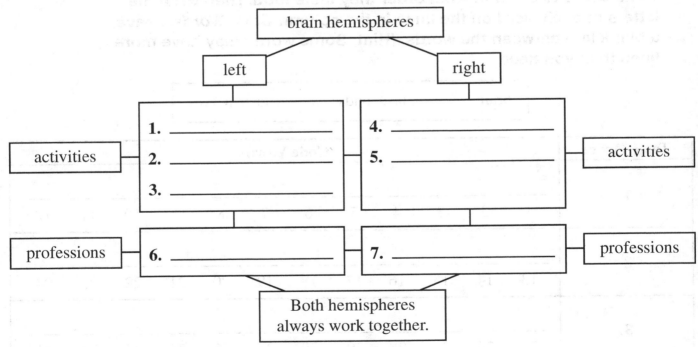

brain hemispheres

left   right

activities
1. _____   4. _____
2. _____   5. _____   activities
3. _____

professions
6. _____   7. _____   professions

Both hemispheres
always work together.

Health, Nutrition, and P.E. 5–6, SV 1419023608

Name _____ Date _____

The Integumentary System

The **integumentary system** is the group of tissues and organs that protect the body. The skin, hair, and nails are part of this system. You can use an apple to find out how the skin protects the body from disease.

 Materials

two small paper plates, crayon or marking pen, two fresh apples, one rotten apple, plastic knife

 Do This

1. Label one of the paper plates *uncut skin.* Label the other one *cut skin.* Place a fresh apple on each paper plate.
2. Cut a badly spoiled piece off the rotten apple. Cut a small piece of the skin off the apple labeled *cut skin.* Rub the piece of rotten apple on the area where the skin has been removed. Some of the rotten apple should stick to the fresh apple. Next, rub the same piece of the rotten apple on the apple labeled *uncut skin.*
3. Throw away the small pieces of the apples and the rest of the rotten apple. Clean up your area and wash your hands.
4. Put the paper plates with the apples aside. Observe the cut and uncut apples each day for one week. Record your observations in a chart on another piece of paper.

** SUPER IDEA **

Take a digital photo of each apple each day for seven days. Make a computer presentation using the photos. Explain what happens in each photo. Share your presentation with your class.

Answer these questions.

1. Describe what happened to the cut and uncut apples. How can you explain the difference in the two apples?

   _____

   _____

2. How is your skin like the skin of an apple?

   _____

   _____

Unit 1: Health
Health, Nutrition, and P.E. 5–6, SV 1419023608

The Endocrine System

How tall are you going to get? How does your body stay warm? Why does a boy's voice change when he is 12 or 13? All these activities are controlled by organs called **glands**. Your glands keep many body functions running smoothly. These glands also help your body to react as it should.

Your **endocrine system** is made up of ductless glands. Glands make special chemicals that bring messages to every part of your body. These chemical messengers are called **hormones**. The hormones produced by ductless glands flow directly from the glands into your bloodstream. Each hormone controls different activities in the body. The tissues affected by endocrine hormones are called **target tissues**.

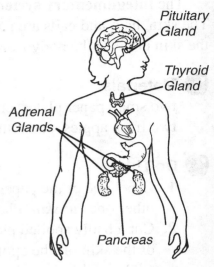

The Endocrine System

The pancreas is a gland that helps control the blood sugar level in your body. Your pancreas secretes a hormone called **insulin**. The primary target tissue of the pancreas is the liver.

The **thyroid gland** has several functions. It controls your **metabolism** and energy levels. The thyroid gland also controls growth and development of the body. The thyroid gland secretes the hormone thyroxine. Thyroxine helps the body determine your food intake requirements. With too much of this hormone, the body releases a lot of energy. The heart speeds up. Body temperature goes up. The person with too much of this hormone may be nervous and lose weight. Target tissues of the thyroid include your small intestine.

Write complete sentences to answer the questions.

1. What is the function of hormones? _____

_____

2. What are target tissues? _____

_____

3. What is the target tissue of the pancreas? _____

_____

4. What are the functions of the thyroid gland? _____

_____

_____

Name _____ Date _____

Hormones and Glands

Glands produce chemicals called **hormones** that control many body functions. These hormones make your body grow and develop. Glands put hormones into the blood. Then the blood carries the hormones to parts of the body where they work.

Two glands help your body grow. The **pituitary gland** makes a hormone that is carried by the blood to the bones. This hormone makes the long bones of the skeleton grow. It helps you reach your adult size. The thyroid gland controls how fast you use food and change it into energy.

Have you ever been frightened or needed to run from danger? A sudden burst of energy often happens in response to stress or danger. This burst of energy comes from **adrenalin**. Adrenalin is produced by the **adrenal glands**. The next time you are startled, feel your heartbeat. How is it different from normal?

Other glands make **sex hormones**. These hormones control the development of male and female sex characteristics. In girls, the sex glands are the **ovaries**. They make breasts develop and hips widen. In boys, the sex glands are the **testes**. They make the voice deepen and body hair grow. In girls, changes in sex characteristics happen between 10 and 16 years of age. Boys change between 12 and 18. This time of change is called **puberty**. It is the stage between childhood and adulthood.

Write words from the box to complete the sentences.

glands	ovaries	pituitary gland
hormones	puberty	adrenalin

1. Chemicals that bring messages to every part of the body are _____.

2. The _____ produces a hormone that makes bones grow.

3. Hormones are made in organs called _____.

4. _____ causes a burst of energy that helps you react to stress or danger.

5. The stage between childhood and adulthood is called _____.

6. In girls, the sex glands are the _____.

Health, Nutrition, and P.E. 5–6, SV 1419023608

Name _____ Date _____

The Reproductive System

Most organisms **reproduce** sexually. In humans, this is the function of the **reproductive system**. In **sexual reproduction**, cells from two parents unite to form one cell, called a **zygote**. The zygote contains **chromosomes** from both the female parent and the male parent. A chromosome is a threadlike strand inside a cell's nucleus that is made up of **DNA**. Nearly all human body cells have 46 chromosomes each. If a body cell has more or fewer than 46 chromosomes, it won't function properly.

Meiosis

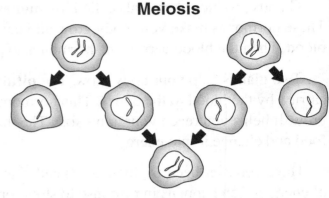

The cells at the top of the diagram are body cells. The cells in the center of the diagram are reproductive cells. Because of meiosis, the reproductive cells have half the number of chromosomes that are in body cells. The cell at the bottom of the diagram is a zygote, with the same number of chromosomes as in body cells.

If two body cells were to unite, the zygote they formed would have 92 chromosomes. Every body cell would then have 92 chromosomes, instead of 46. In the next generation, the zygote and all the body cells would each have 184 chromosomes, and so on. With each new generation, the number of chromosomes would double.

This never happens, though, because the human body produces **reproductive cells**, which have only 23 chromosomes each—half the number of chromosomes found in body cells. **Meiosis** is the process that reduces the number of chromosomes in reproductive cells.

In the first stage of meiosis, the cell copies its chromosomes and divides. Both of the new cells have 46 chromosomes. In the second stage of meiosis, the two cells divide again. However, this time they do not copy their chromosomes first. Each of the four new cells is a reproductive cell, or **gamete**. Gametes have half the number of chromosomes that are in a body cell.

🍎 **Darken the circle by the answer that best completes each sentence.**

1. In sexual reproduction, cells from two parents unite to form a _____.
   Ⓐ gamete   Ⓑ zygote   Ⓒ chromosome   Ⓓ meiosis

2. A _____ is a threadlike strand inside a cell's nucleus that is made up of DNA.
   Ⓐ gamete   Ⓑ zygote   Ⓒ chromosome   Ⓓ meiosis

3. Nearly all human body cells have _____ chromosomes each.
   Ⓐ 46   Ⓑ 92   Ⓒ 184   Ⓓ 7

4. A reproductive cell is also called a _____.
   Ⓐ gamete   Ⓑ zygote   Ⓒ chromosome   Ⓓ meiosis

     Health, Nutrition, and P.E. 5–6, SV 1419023608

Reproduction

The word *reproduce* means "to make more." People reproduce by making babies. You started life as one cell. This cell formed when sperm from your father fertilized an egg from your mother. Then you started to grow inside your mother. Your mother was **pregnant**. But how did you develop?

Blood vessels from the **uterus** and the developing **fetus** grow to form a tissue called the **placenta**. As more of the cells of the fetus grow, some of the cells form a tube. This tube is the **umbilical cord**. It attaches the fetus to the placenta.

When the mother eats, food is broken down into tiny particles. These particles flow through her blood to the placenta. Then they move through the umbilical cord and into the fetus. That's how the fetus gets food, oxygen, and water. Waste from the fetus passes into the mother through the placenta.

After about 9 months, the baby is ready to be born. The baby moves down through the **birth canal** to the outside of the mother's body. The doctor cuts the umbilical cord. The place where it was attached becomes the baby's **navel**, or belly button. The baby now breathes and eats outside its mother's body.

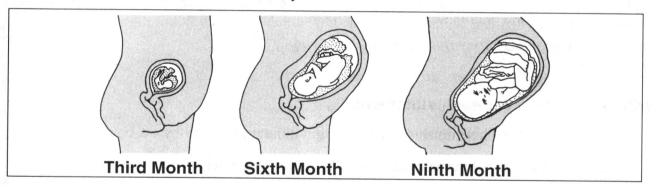

Third Month   **Sixth Month**   **Ninth Month**

 Write the correct answer from the ( ) to complete each sentence.

1. When the father's sperm fertilizes the mother's egg, the mother becomes

   _____. (sleepy, pregnant, placenta)

2. A baby grows for about _____ before it is born.
   (1 year, 6 months, 9 months)

3. A placenta is made of _____. (a sperm cell, blood vessels, hair)

4. Food from the mother passes through the _____ and into the fetus through the umbilical cord. (placenta, birth canal, pregnant)

5. After the baby is born, the place where the umbilical cord was attached becomes

   the baby's _____. (placenta, head, navel)

Health, Nutrition, and P.E. 5–6, SV 1419023608

Getting Traits from Parents

You might have the same color hair as your mother. Or you might be as tall as your father. Why do children look a lot like their parents?

You start life with one cell from your mother and one from your father. These cells have all the information you need to grow. This information is carried in parts of the cells called chromosomes. Most cells have 46 chromosomes. You get 23 from your mother and 23 from your father.

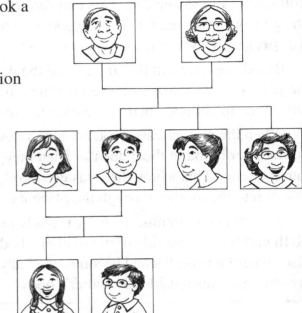

Chromosomes have smaller parts called **genes**. Genes determine whether you will be a boy or a girl. They also determine your **traits**. Features like hair color and height are traits. The passing of traits from parents to children is called **heredity**. Each person has a special set of traits. Only identical twins have exactly the same traits. Identical twins form when a fertilized egg divides into two parts. Each part develops into a baby.

Write *true* or *false* for each statement.

_____ **1.** Genes determine whether you will be a girl or a boy.

_____ **2.** Genes have smaller parts called chromosomes.

_____ **3.** Traits are features like height and hair color.

_____ **4.** The passing of traits from parents to children is called traiting.

_____ **5.** Only identical twins have the same set of traits.

Use each word to write a sentence about heredity.

6. traits _____

_____

7. heredity _____

_____

Name _____ Date _____

What Do You Know About Heredity?

Heredity is the passing on of traits from parents to children. Many people believe things about heredity without really knowing whether they are true. Find out how much you know.

Read each statement. If the statement is true, write *T* in the blank. If the statement is false, write *F* in the blank.

_____ **1.** Each parent gives one-half of a child's genetic makeup.

_____ **2.** Before birth, inherited traits may be changed by the stars, the moon, or the planets.

_____ **3.** A child may have traits that the parent doesn't show.

_____ **4.** Many of a person's inherited traits cannot be seen.

_____ **5.** If a person loses an arm in an accident, his or her children may be born with only one arm.

_____ **6.** If a woman wants her child to be an artist, she should take up painting before the child is born.

_____ **7.** Some inherited traits are affected by a person's blood.

_____ **8.** A child may have a trait that is a blend of the parents' traits.

_____ **9.** A child will be more like a parent who is strong-willed than one who is not.

_____ **10.** Parents who are tall will always have children who are tall.

Health, Nutrition, and P.E. 5–6, SV 1419023608

Name _____ Date _____

Comparing Human Traits

🍎 **Use the chart to find your combination of the five traits.**

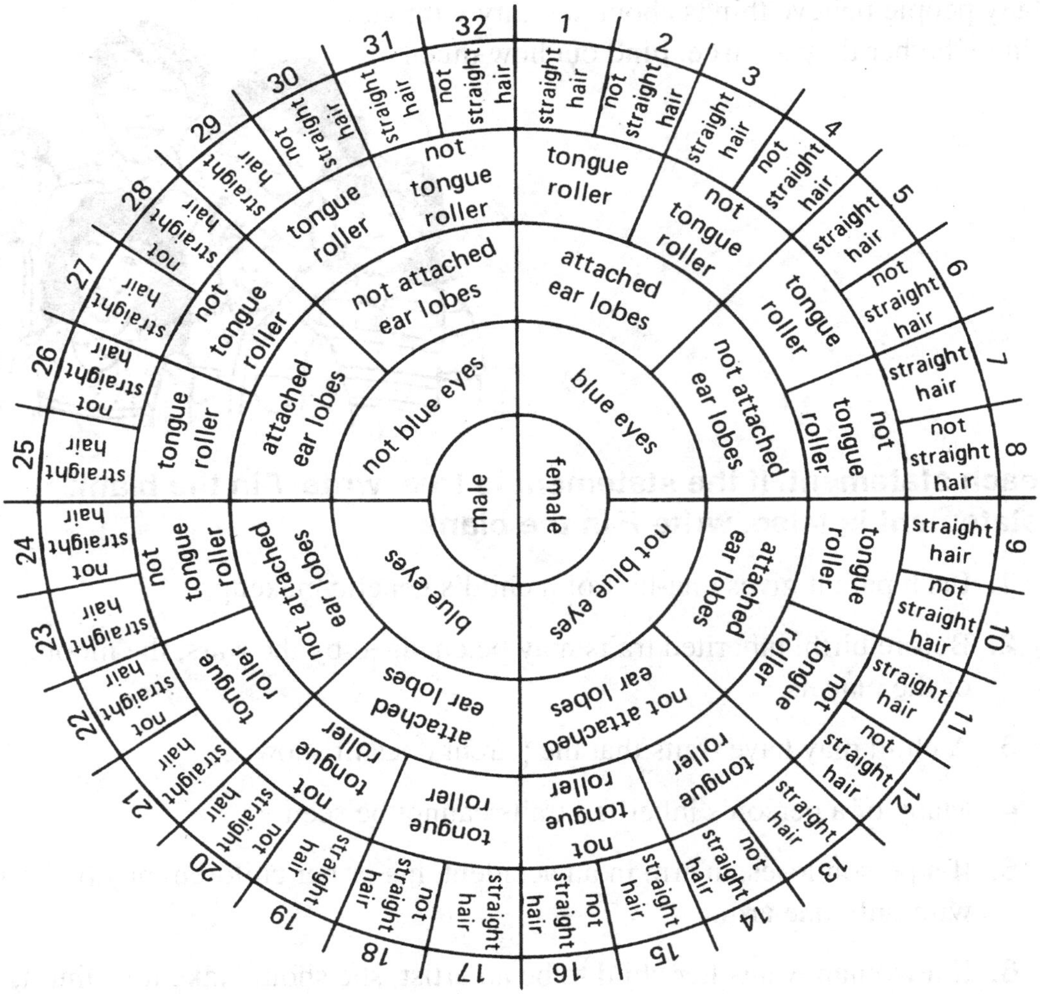

🍎 **Locate *male* or *female* on the chart. Move out one ring to eye color. Continue until you reach the number on the outside edge.**

1. What is the number for your combination of five traits?

   _____

2. How many other students have the same trait number?

   _____

3. How many have different trait numbers?

   _____

Unit 1: Health

Health, Nutrition, and P.E. 5–6, SV 1419023608

Name _____ Date _____

Good Hygiene

An important part of staying healthy is keeping your teeth and your body clean. It is important to keep the germs and bacteria that come in contact with your body from spreading. This is why you wash your body and hair. It is very important that you wash your hands whenever you handle garbage or raw meats (such as when you make a hamburger) and each time you use the bathroom. Germs can be spread easily from person to person, too. If you cough or sneeze without covering your mouth, germs fly out into the air and onto other people. If you cover your mouth, the germs are contained, and it is less likely that you will spread your germs to someone else. It is not a good idea to share straws, cups, combs, or hats, either. Germs can be passed from one person to the next this way, as well.

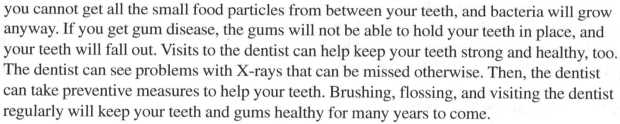

Brushing your teeth keeps bacteria from living in your mouth. Bacteria eat small particles of food that are in your mouth. Acids can form that eat into the enamel that protects your teeth. When acid eats into your teeth, decay begins, and you will get cavities. So it is important that you brush your teeth after every meal. Just brushing is not enough, however. If you do not floss, you cannot get all the small food particles from between your teeth, and bacteria will grow anyway. If you get gum disease, the gums will not be able to hold your teeth in place, and your teeth will fall out. Visits to the dentist can help keep your teeth strong and healthy, too. The dentist can see problems with X-rays that can be missed otherwise. Then, the dentist can take preventive measures to help your teeth. Brushing, flossing, and visiting the dentist regularly will keep your teeth and gums healthy for many years to come.

Good hygiene helps to keep you healthy and feeling good. It makes you look and smell better, too! Do you have good hygiene habits?

Answer the following questions to see if you need to improve your hygiene.

	Yes	No
1. Do you take a bath or shower every day?		
2. Do you brush your teeth after each meal?		
3. Do you brush your teeth at least twice a day?		
4. Do you floss your teeth every day?		
5. Do you visit the dentist regularly?		
6. Do you cover your mouth when you sneeze or cough?		
7. Do you wash your hands after using the bathroom?		
8. Do you wash your hands after handling garbage or raw meats?		
9. Do you share combs, hats, or other items that go in the hair?		
10. Do you share cups, straws, or other eating utensils?		

If you answered "yes" to 1–8, and "no" to 9 and 10, good for you! You have good hygiene habits already! If not, try to improve your habits, and take the test again in two weeks!

Health, Nutrition, and P.E. 5–6, SV 1419023608

Preventing Disease

How can you keep from getting **diseases** caused by bacteria or **viruses**? You can start by taking care of your body. If you are tired or do not eat well, your body defenses will not work at their best. Look at the table on this page for some ways to stay healthy.

Suppose you get a cold or the flu. Try not to spread it to others. Stay at home for a day or two so other people do not catch your cold. Cover your nose and mouth when you cough or sneeze.

People can also lower their chances of getting **disorders** like heart disease. They can eat a balanced diet that is low in fats. They can exercise. Exercise helps keep heart muscles strong. It also helps a person lose weight. People who are overweight have a greater chance of getting heart disease. Regular visits to a doctor are important, too. In these checkups, a doctor can find **high blood pressure** and other signs of heart disease. A doctor can also find early signs of cancer.

SOME WAYS TO STAY HEALTHY

1. Eat a balanced diet.
2. Get about 8 hours of sleep every night.
3. Exercise for about 20 minutes 3 times a week.
4. Wash your hands before you eat and after going to the bathroom.
5. Bathe or shower often.
6. Do not use the dishes, glasses, towels, or other objects of a person with a cold or the flu.
7. Get regular checkups from a doctor.

Write *true* or *false* for each statement.

_____ 1. Your body defenses work best when you are tired.

_____ 2. You can't lower your chances of getting heart disease.

_____ 3. Exercise helps keep heart muscles strong.

_____ 4. During a checkup, a doctor can find early signs of cancer.

_____ 5. You should cover your nose and mouth when you sneeze or cough.

_____ 6. Regular exercise is not a good way to stay healthy.

Health and Smoking

Every day, millions of Americans use **tobacco**. Some people chew it in the form of chewing tobacco. A few inhale it as a powder known as snuff. But most people—more than 46 million adults—smoke tobacco in cigarettes, cigars, and pipes.

Smoking became common hundreds of years ago. At that time, people did not know that the smoking habit could harm their health. Today, people have much information about the effects of smoking. They know that smoking can increase the heartbeat. It can produce a bad cough or make breathing difficult. Smoking destroys vitamins in the body. It even harms people who breathe in the smoke from another person's cigarette.

People are also given warnings about the more serious effects of smoking. By law, all cigarette packs must carry warnings about the danger of smoking. Smoking can lead to diseases of the circulatory system and the respiratory system. Every year, about 440,000 people in the United States die from diseases related to smoking. If people know about these effects, why do they smoke?

People smoke for many reasons. Ads in magazines show smokers as healthy people having fun. Young people may start to smoke because they think it makes them look older. They may also smoke because their friends smoke.

Yet more and more people today are listening to the warnings. They want to stay healthy. One of the ways to stay healthy is to choose not to smoke.

Write complete sentences to answer the questions.

1. What are three effects that smoking has on the body?

_____

_____

_____

2. What is one reason that young people start to smoke?

_____

_____

Health, Nutrition, and P.E. 5–6, SV 1419023608

The Cost of Smoking

All forms of tobacco contain **nicotine**. Nicotine stimulates the pleasure centers of the brain. Tobacco users get a feeling of pleasure that lasts several seconds each time they use tobacco. The more tobacco they use, however, the sicker they will be over time. Nicotine puts stress on the heart and raises blood pressure. **Carbon monoxide** and **tars** in cigarette smoke will also damage a smoker's heart, lungs, and air passages. This can lead to more colds and sore throats as well as more serious diseases, such as **bronchitis**, **emphysema**, and **lung cancer**. Many of these diseases can be fatal.

Smoking tobacco is not only dangerous to your health, but it is also expensive. Answer the questions and find out why.

1. What is the cost of a pack of cigarettes? _____

2. If a person smokes one pack of cigarettes each day, how much will that person spend in one year? _____

3. If the same person starts smoking at age 16 and smokes until age 55, how much will be spent on cigarettes? Assume that the price stays the same.

    _____

4. There are 20 cigarettes in a pack. How many cigarettes does the one-pack-per-day smoker smoke in one year?

    _____

5. How many cigarettes does the same smoker smoke in 40 years?

    _____

6. If one cigarette shortens a smoker's life by 5.5 minutes, by how many minutes has the smoker shortened his or her life?

    _____

7. By about how many years has the smoker's life been shortened?

    _____

8. Can you think of other reasons that smoking costs money? What are they?

    _____

    _____

    _____

Health, Nutrition, and P.E. 5–6, SV 1419023608

The Effects of Alcohol

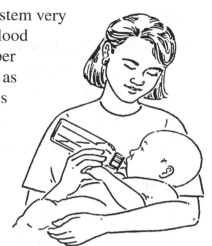

When a person drinks alcohol, the alcohol is absorbed into the system very quickly and travels to the brain. If drinks are taken too quickly, the blood alcohol content (BAC) is raised. BAC means the amount of alcohol per 100 units of blood. The chart below shows what happens to the BAC as a person drinks. When this content is very high, it means the person is "drunk." A person should not drive a car or do anything that might cause danger to himself or herself or to others. Sometimes when a person drinks too much, the next day he or she has a hangover.

Alcoholism is a disease. Alcoholics are not able to control their drinking. They are often drunk, which hurts them, their families, and their friends. They may also hurt their health. Sometimes they end up with a condition called cirrhosis, a scarring of the liver, which can lead to death.

There are times when even a little alcohol can be harmful to a person. For example, if a pregnant woman drinks, it can cause fetal alcohol syndrome (FAS) in her baby. FAS can cause a variety of birth defects in a baby.

It is important to remember that drinking does not make a person a grown-up. It is all right to choose not to drink. It is important not to be pressured into drinking if you don't want to. Remember, the choice is yours!

BAC for a Person Weighing 120 Pounds		
Number of Drinks in One Hour	BAC	Effects
1 2	.04 .08	Alcohol affects thinking and emotions. Good judgment and self-control decrease.
3 4 5	.11 .15 .19	It becomes difficult to think clearly. Even simple movements become difficult.
6 7 8	.23 .26 .30	Speech becomes slurred. Hearing and vision are impaired.
9 10	.34 .38	The person can no longer stand. There may be vomiting and unconsciousness.

Go on to the next page.

The Effects of Alcohol, p. 2

Across

2. Women who drink too much during pregnancy may give birth to babies with _____ syndrome.

3. The effect of alcohol on the brain is related to the body's ability to _____ it.

4. The initials that define the amount of alcohol per 100 units of blood are _____.

7. Drinking too much may cause a _____ with a headache or stomachache.

Down

1. _____ is a disease in which the person is unable to control his or her drinking.

5. Scarring of the liver, often caused by drinking, is called _____.

6. A person with a high BAC is said to be _____.

Health and Drug Abuse

A **drug** is a substance other than food that changes the way the body works. You have read how alcohol changes the way the body works. Alcohol is a drug. Some drugs, like alcohol, are legal. You can buy legal drugs like aspirin in stores. Other drugs are illegal. They can be bought only on the street. Some legal drugs are **prescribed** by doctors. These drugs help sick people get well, but even these drugs can be **abused**.

Barbiturates are legal drugs. They slow down the nervous system. For this reason, they are known as "downers." Doctors may prescribe barbiturates for people who have trouble sleeping. Taking barbiturates when a doctor has not prescribed them is abusing them. An **overdose**, or taking too much at one time, can kill a person. Mixing barbiturates and alcohol can also lead to death.

Amphetamines are legal drugs that speed up the nervous system. For this reason, they are called "speed" or "uppers." Doctors may prescribe amphetamines for people who need to lose weight. Other people take the drug for the excited feeling it gives them. As the drug wears off, the drug user feels bad and wants more to feel better. Barbiturates and amphetamines change the speed of the heartbeat. When these drugs are abused, they can cause heart failure.

Marijuana is the most widely used illegal drug in the United States. It is also known as "pot," "grass," or "weed." It is usually smoked. Smoking marijuana has some of the same harmful effects as smoking tobacco. Smoking marijuana can also affect a person's memory and learning.

 Match the words in the left column and the descriptions that match them in the right column. Write the letter of the description on the correct line.

_____ **1.** drug   **A.** speed up the nervous system

_____ **2.** to abuse   **B.** an illegal drug that is usually smoked

_____ **3.** barbiturates   **C.** to use something the wrong way

_____ **4.** overdose   **D.** slow down the nervous system

_____ **5.** amphetamines   **E.** too much at one time

_____ **6.** marijuana   **F.** changes the way the body works

Health, Nutrition, and P.E. 5–6, SV 1419023608

Name _____   Date _____

What Would You Do?

🍎 **Read the paragraphs. Circle the letter of the correct answer to each question. Then, in the space provided, tell why you chose your answer.**

1. Clara and her family moved into their house last week. They found a medicine cabinet filled with bottles of medicine. There was a note taped to the cabinet from the person who had lived in the house before them. It said, "I don't want any of these things. They are yours if you want them." Clara told her family that she did not think they should use someone else's medicine. What should Clara's family do?

   A. They should save the OTC (over-the-counter) medicines but throw away the prescription medicines.
   B. They should keep all the medicines in case they need them later.
   C. They should throw away all the medicines.

   Why? _____

   _____

   _____

   _____

2. Eleven-year-old Dennis woke up with a stuffy nose and watery, itchy eyes. In the past these symptoms were caused by his allergies. His dad usually gave him an over-the-counter medicine kept in the bathroom medicine cabinet. Dennis knows right where it is. What should Dennis do?

   A. He should take the medicine.
   B. He should take the medicine only if he is sure he is correctly following the package.
   C. He should wait until his father or another adult can talk to a doctor or decide what he should do.

   Why? _____

   _____

   _____

   _____

Health, Nutrition, and P.E. 5–6, SV 1419023608

Name _____ Date _____

Identifying a Stressful Situation

 The chart below lists 18 possible sources of stress. As you read each source, think about what it means to you. Then, number a piece of paper from 1 to 18. Now, list the sources of stress in order from those you find to be most stressful to those you find to be least stressful. (The most stressful will be number 1.)

Possible Sources of Stress	
Not having done your homework	Going on a trip
Having an argument at home	Imagining what others think of you
Meeting new people	Being in a sports competition
Taking a test	Giving a speech
Getting sick	Moving into a new neighborhood
Being called on in class	Being hot, cold, hungry, or tired
Writing a difficult report	Being late for class
Learning a new skill	Being too busy
Attending the first day of school	Receiving a report card

 Answer these questions.

1. Which of these sources of stress have you actually experienced lately?

_____

_____

2. Which of these sources of stress have you never experienced?

_____

_____

3. Explain why you find each of the first three sources on your list to be stressful.

_____

_____

4. What can you do to lessen stress from your first three sources?

_____

_____

Health, Nutrition, and P.E. 5–6, SV 1419023608

Teacher Resource

Obesity has become a major concern of both children and adults in the United States. The large serving sizes of fast foods combined with a sedentary lifestyle are the prime reasons for increased weight. It is important for children to recognize that they can make choices that will help them live healthy lives. They need to learn the connections between what they eat and the way they look and feel. They need to have the basic information that will help them make good food choices.

The revised food pyramid offers a suggestion for maintaining a healthy lifestyle. It recommends serving sizes for each food group and oils based on individual needs. Eating the right amount of foods from each group every day provides a balanced diet. Eating too many foods from one group or not enough of another can lead to deficiencies or weight problems. Although vitamin supplements can help with these deficiencies, vitamins are best absorbed in the body naturally through the digestion of the foods that contain them.

Nutrition

The body needs to receive certain nutrients in order to grow and to stay healthy. These nutrients are broken down into six types: carbohydrates, proteins, fat, vitamins, minerals, and water.

Carbohydrates are sugars and starches. Sugars, such as fruits and honey, give the body quick energy, while the starches, such as bread, cereal, and rice, give the body stored energy.

Proteins come from foods such as milk, cheese, lean meat, fish, peas, and beans; they help the body to repair itself. Proteins are used by the body to build muscle and bone, and they give the body energy.

Fat is important for energy, too, and it helps to keep the body warm. If the body does not use the fats put into it, it will store the fat. Fats come from foods such as meat, milk, butter, oil, and nuts.

Vitamins are important to the body in many ways. Vitamins help the other nutrients in a person's body work together. Lack of certain vitamins can cause serious illnesses. Vitamin A, for example, which can be obtained from foods such as broccoli, carrots, and liver, helps with eyesight. Vitamin B, from green leafy vegetables, eggs, and milk, helps with growth and energy.

Minerals can be found in foods such as milk, vegetables, seafood, and raisins. They help the body grow. Calcium is a mineral that helps make strong bones, and iron is needed for healthy red blood.

Water makes up most of the human body and helps to keep the body's temperature regulated. People should drink several glasses of water each day.

The Food Pyramid

A new food pyramid has recently been approved. Since each person is different in terms of age, sex, and exercise levels, the new food pyramid suggests daily dietary needs based on these characteristics. The web site www.MyPyramid.gov not only gives serving suggestions and caloric intake, but the site offers a wealth of information, including a reminder to exercise daily. Students can use the web site two ways. They can use the site on a one-time basis, and their input information is not saved. They can also register with the web site, and then their input information can be saved to track their food intake or physical activity over a period of time.

The five food groups plus oils guidelines have changed slightly. Point out that the width of the food group stripes on the pyramid suggests how much food a person should choose from each group. Encourage children to choose more foods from the food groups with the widest stripes. Encourage children to read food labels.

Grains are made from plants, such as wheat, corn, rice, oats, and barley. Servings of grains are given in ounces.

Vegetables include plants as well as 100 percent juice. They can be served in any manner, raw or cooked. There are five vegetable subgroups: dark green, orange, dry beans and peas, starch, and other vegetables. The serving size for vegetables is given in cups.

Fruits, like vegetables, can be fresh, canned, or 100 percent juice. Eating a wide variety of colorful fruits is highly recommended. Serving sizes are also in cups.

Oils are to be used sparingly. We all need some oil. Oils are found in butter, margarine, nuts, fish, and liquid oils such as corn, soybean, canola, and olive oil. Serving sizes are given in teaspoons.

Milk includes such foods as milk, cheese, yogurt, and ice cream. Skim and low-fat products are recommended to reduce the oil intake. Servings are given in cups.

Meat and Beans include fish, poultry, beef, eggs, nuts, and dried beans such as navy beans and kidney beans. Serving sizes are given in ounces.

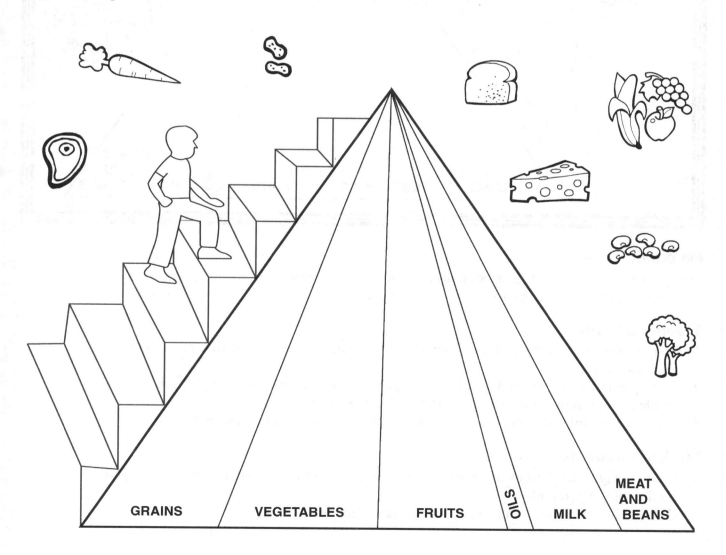

GRAINS   VEGETABLES   FRUITS   OILS   MILK   MEAT AND BEANS

Bulletin Board: Eating the Pyramid Way

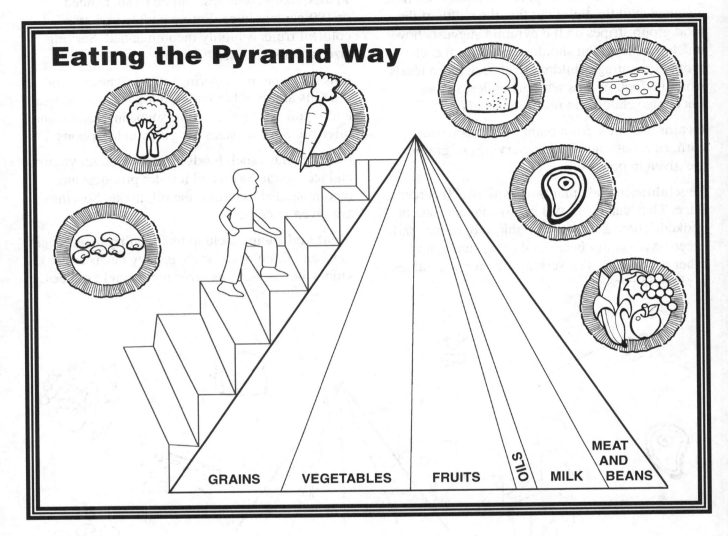

Materials

craft paper   large paper plates   markers   stapler
recycled magazines   scissors   glue

Teacher Directions

1. Prepare a bulletin board with the desired color of craft paper. Add the title "Eating the Pyramid Way."
2. Draw the new food pyramid on white craft paper. Color and cut out the pyramid.
3. Staple the pyramid in the center of the board. Label each section.
4. Staple the completed paper plate meals to the board in a pleasing arrangement.

Student Directions

1. Cut out magazine pictures that show healthy foods. Choose a food that comes from each section of the pyramid.
2. Glue the food pictures to a plate to show a balanced meal.

Health, Nutrition, and P.E. 5–6, SV 1419023608

Name _____ Date _____

The Food Pyramid Web Site Activity 1

There is a web site that tells about the food pyramid. It will tell you how much of each food to eat so you can be healthy. The man on the steps will also help you remember to exercise every day. You can visit the site at this address: **www.MyPyramid.gov**

 Follow the steps to find the food pyramid that is just right for you.

Step 1: Type in this address in the address bar of your Internet browser: **www.MyPyramid.gov**

Step 2: Look on the right side of the screen. Find the box that says **My Pyramid Plan**.

Step 3: Find the word **Age**. Type your age in the box under the word.

Step 4: Find the word **Sex**. Click on the arrow. If you are a boy, choose **Male**. If you are a girl, choose **Female**.

Step 5: Find the words **Physical Activity**. Go down to the Select menu and click on the arrow. How much exercise do you get every day? Choose the words.

Step 6: Click on the word **SUBMIT**. Watch the screen change.

 Look at the numbers that tell how much of each food you should eat every day. Write the numbers in the chart below. The chart does not tell how many teaspoons of oil to eat. To find that information, you need to look below the chart.

Food Group	How Much to Eat
Grains	_____ ounces
Vegetables	_____ cups
Fruits	_____ cups
Oils	_____ teaspoons
Milk	_____ cups
Meat and Beans	_____ ounces

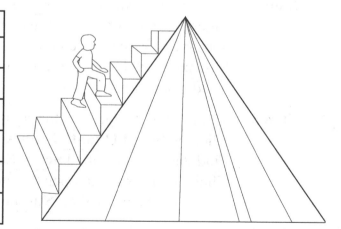

 Write complete sentences to answer the question.

How do the recommended amounts compare with the amounts of food you eat?

_____

_____

Name _____ Date _____

The Food Pyramid Web Site Activity 2

There is a web site that tells about the food pyramid. It will tell you how much of each food to eat so you can be healthy. The man on the steps will also help you remember to exercise every day. You can visit the site at this address: **www.MyPyramid.gov**

Follow the directions to track your food intake for a day.

Step 1: First, make a list of everything you eat for one day. You will use the list to see how healthy your diet is.

Step 2: Type in this address in the address bar of your Internet browser: **www.MyPyramid.gov**

Step 3: Look on the right side of the screen.
Find the box that says **My Pyramid Tracker**.
Click on the words **My Pyramid Tracker**.

Step 4: You will go to another page. Move down to the bottom of the page and click on **Check It Out**.

Step 5: You will go to another page. Fill in the requested information.
Then click on **Save Today's Changes**.

Step 6: Then click on **Proceed to Food Intake**. You will go to another page.

Step 7: Put the cursor in the **Enter Food Item** search box.
Enter the first item on your list, and click on **Search**. A list of foods will appear below the Search box.
Find the food that most closely matches your food item. Click on **Add** beside that choice.

Step 8: The food will appear on the right side of the screen.
Click on **Select Quantity**. You will go to another page.
Find the heading called **Select Serving Size**.
Click on the arrow to open the menu, and click on the correct serving size.
Then find the box called **Number of Servings**. Enter a number in the box.

Step 9: When you finish entering the number of servings, click on **Enter Foods**.
Continue to enter foods until you have completed your list.

Go on to the next page.

Health, Nutrition, and P.E. 5–6, SV 1419023608

Name _____ Date _____

The Food Pyramid Web Site Activity 2, p. 2

Step 10: When you complete your food list, you should be on the servings page.
Click on **Save & Analyze**.
You will go to another page called **Analyze Your Food Intake**.
Find the box called **Meeting 2005 Dietary Guidelines**.
Click on **Calculate DG Comparison**. You will go to another page.

Step 11: Click on the circle by **Maintains Your Current Weight**.
Then click on **Go!**
You will go to another page. This new page will have a chart that shows the foods you should eat, the foods you entered, and the recommended amounts you should eat. The page will also have happy faces and sad faces. If you click on the faces, you will get more information about a good diet.

Step 12: With permission, print out your Dietary Recommendations page.

Use your Dietary Recommendations page to answer the questions.

1. How many happy faces did you receive? _____

   How many sad faces did you receive? _____

2. How closely did your amount of fruits eaten compare to the recommended amounts?

   _____

   _____

3. Do you think you have a healthy diet? Explain why or why not.

   _____

   _____

Health, Nutrition, and P.E. 5–6, SV 1419023608

Name _____   Date _____

The Food Pyramid Web Site Activity 2, p. 3

There is a web site that tells about the food pyramid. It will tell you how much of each food to eat so you can be healthy. The man on the steps will also help you remember to exercise every day. You can visit the site at this address: **www.MyPyramid.gov**

 Follow the steps to track your nutrient intake for a day.

Step 1: After you print out your Dietary Recommendations page, click on **Nutrient Intakes** at the bottom of the page. You will go to another page. This page will contain a Nutrient Intakes chart. On the left are the nutrients, in the middle are the amounts of nutrients you ate, and on the right are the recommended amounts of the nutrients.

Step 2: With permission, print out your Nutrient Intakes page.

Follow the directions to find how your diet compares to the recommended diet.

Step 3: After you print out your Nutrient Intakes page, click on **MyPyramid Recommendation** at the bottom of the page. You will go to another page. This page will contain a comparison of your food intake with the recommended diet. You will see some bar graphs at the top and a chart at the bottom.

Step 4: With permission, print out your Comparison page.

Use your Nutrient Intakes and Comparison pages to answer the questions.

1. How many total calories did you take in? _____

   What was your recommended amount? _____

2. How many grams of protein did you take in? _____

   What was your recommended amount? _____

3. How many grams of total fat did you take in? _____

   What was your recommended amount? _____

4. How did your milk intake compare with the recommendation? _____

   _____

5. How did your vegetables intake compare with the recommendation? _____

   _____

6. In what ways can you improve your diet? _____

Health, Nutrition, and P.E. 5–6, SV 1419023608

Name _____ Date _____

The Food Pyramid Web Site Activity 3

There is a web site that tells how much physical activity you should get. You can visit the site at this address: **www.MyPyramid.gov**

Follow the steps to find out about your physical activity level.

Step 1: First, make a list of all your physical activities for one day. You will use the list to see how active you are.

Step 2: Type in this address in the address bar of your Internet browser: **www.MyPyramid.gov**

Step 3: Look on the right side of the screen. Find the box that says **My Pyramid Tracker**. Click on the words **My Pyramid Tracker**. You will go to another page. Move down to the bottom of the page and click on **Check It Out**.

Step 4: You will go to another page. Fill in the requested information. Then click on **Save Today's Changes**.

Step 5: Then click on **Proceed to Physical Activity**. You will go to another page.

Step 6: Find the **Enter Activity Type** box on the left. You can either select from a list of activities or type in your activity. Enter the first item on your list. A list of activities will appear below the Search box. Find the activity that most closely matches your activity. Click on the activity. Then click on **Add Activity** below the choices.

Step 7: The activity will appear on the right side of the screen. Click on **Select Duration**. You will go to another page. Find the box called **Select Duration (in minutes)**. Enter the number of minutes you did the activity in the box.

Step 8: When you finish entering the number of minutes, click on **Enter Activities**. Continue to enter activities until you have completed your list.

Step 9: When you complete your activities list, you should be on the duration page. Click on **Save & Analyze**. You will go to another page that will show your total minutes of physical activity. Click on **Analyze**. You will go to another page called **Physical Activity Results**. Find the **Result Summary** chart at the bottom of the page.

Step 10: With permission, print out the **Physical Activity Results** page.

Use your Result Summary chart to answer the questions.

1. How many minutes of physical activity did you have? _____

2. How many calories did you use in your physical activity? _____

3. What was your Physical Activity Score? _____

4. What was your Physical Activity Assessment? _____

5. Do you think you need more physical activities? _____

6. What can you do to improve your Physical Activity Score? _____

Health, Nutrition, and P.E. 5–6, SV 1419023608

Nutrients

Your body needs nutrients in order to grow and stay healthy. A balanced diet provides all the nutrients you need. Here are the basic nutrients your body needs.

- **Carbohydrates** give the body stored energy.
- **Proteins** help the body to repair itself and give the body energy.
- **Fat** is important for energy, too, and it helps to keep the body warm.
- **Vitamins** are important to the body in many ways. Vitamins help the other nutrients in a person's body work together. They also help the body with growth and energy.
- **Minerals** help the body grow. Calcium is a mineral that helps make strong bones, and iron is needed for healthy red blood.
- **Water** makes up most of the human body and keeps the body's temperature regulated.

Write the letter of each use in the right column in front of the correct nutrient in the left column.

_____ 1. Carbohydrates   **A.** Growth and repair

_____ 2. Fat   **B.** Small amounts for growth and activity

_____ 3. Protein   **C.** To form parts of the body

_____ 4. Vitamins   **D.** Stored energy

_____ 5. Minerals   **E.** Makes up 75 to 80 percent of the body

_____ 6. Water   **F.** Keeps body warm

Name a food source for each nutrient listed above.

7. _____

_____

_____

_____

_____

_____

_____

Counting Calories

A **Calorie** is the unit that measures the amount of energy in food. Fruits and vegetables have smaller amounts of Calories, while desserts have more.

Knowledge about the food you eat is important if you wish to have a balanced diet. You will need diet and health books to obtain this information.

A. Choose six of your favorite foods, and list them in the chart below. Draw a picture of the food, and write down the food group it belongs to.

B. Using the diet and health books, find out the number of Calories in one serving of each food item. Are you consuming more Calories than you need?

Food Item	Picture	Food Group	Number of Calories

73

Name _____ Date _____

How Do You Know If a Food Contains Starch?

Starch is an important part of many foods. It is a carbohydrate and an important part of our diet. Some people, though, must limit the amount of starch they eat. Here is one way to find out if a food contains starch.

Materials

bread	cooked rice	raw potato
apple slice	bologna	butter
wax paper	eyedropper	iodine

CAUTION: Iodine is a poison. It should never be tasted.

Procedure

1. Put a small piece of each food on a piece of wax paper. (You may use the same piece of wax paper to hold all the foods.)
2. Use the eyedropper to place three drops of iodine on each piece of food.
3. If a black spot appears on the food, it contains starch.
4. Make a list of all the foods that contain starch.

Drawing Conclusions

1. Do any of the foods change color?

   _____

   _____

2. What happens to the foods that contain starch?

   _____

   _____

More Ideas for Your Project

- Include your setup and findings in your display. Demonstrate your test for the judges.
- Research to find other foods that contain starch. Include a list in your report.
- How important is starch in your diet? What diseases or medical problems might cause you to limit your starch intake?

Health, Nutrition, and P.E. 5–6, SV 1419023608

Reading a Food Label

 The skill of observation is important when deciding what foods to eat. Read the cereal box shown in the margin, and answer the questions below.

1. How many Calories are in one serving of this cereal without milk? With milk?

   _____

   _____

2. Does this cereal contain more carbohydrates or more fats?

   _____

3. Does this cereal contain more starch or more sugar?

   _____

4. What does RDA mean?

   _____

   _____

5. How much of the U.S. RDA of vitamin A is in $\frac{1}{4}$ cup of cereal?

   _____

6. What minerals are in this cereal?

   _____

   _____

7. Which do you think are the five main ingredients in this cereal?

   _____

   _____

8. According to the cereal box, how could you increase the amount of protein in this cereal?

   _____

   _____

Each serving contains 4 g dietary fiber, including 1 g (2.6% by weight) non-nutritive crude fiber.

NUTRITION INFORMATION PER SERVING

Serving Size: 1/4 cup Raisin Bran (1 ounce bran flakes with 1/3 ounce raisins) alone, and in combination with 1/2 cup Vitamin D fortified whole milk.
Servings Per Container: 15

	Raisin Bran	
	1 oz. Cereal & 1/3 oz. raisins	with 1/2 cup whole milk
Calories	120	190
Protein	3 g	7 g
Carbohydrate	29 g	35 g
Fat	1 g	5 g

PERCENTAGE OF U.S. RECOMMENDED DAILY ALLOWANCE (U.S. RDA)

	Raisin Bran	
	1 oz. Cereal & 1/3 oz. raisins	with 1/2 cup whole milk
Protein	4	15
Vitamin A	25	30
Vitamin C	*	2
Thiamin	25	30
Riboflavin	25	35
Niacin	25	25
Calcium	*	15
Iron	25	25
Vitamin D	10	25
Vitamin B4	25	25
Folic Acid	25	25
Vitamin B12	25	30
Phosphorus	15	25
Magnesium	15	20
Zinc	25	30
Copper	6	6

*Contains less than 2% of the U.S. RDA of these nutrients.

INGREDIENTS: Wheat Bran with other parts of wheat; Raisins; Sugar; Salt; Malt Flavoring; Partially Hydrogenated Vegetable Oil (One or More of: Coconut, Soybean, and Palm); Invert Syrup; Vitamin A Palmitate; Reduced Iron; Zinc Oxide; Niacinamide; Pyridoxine Hydrochloride (B6); Thiamin Hydrochloride (B1); Riboflavin (B2); Folic Acid; Vitamin B12; and Vitamin D2.

CARBOHYDRATE INFORMATION

	Raisin Bran	
	1 oz. Cereal & 1/3 oz. raisins	with 1/2 cup whole milk
Starch and Related Carbohydrates	12 g	12 g
Sucrose and Other Sugars	13 g	19 g
Dietary Fiber	4 g	4 g
Total Carbohydrates	29 g	35 g

Values by Formulation and Analysis.

Health, Nutrition, and P.E. 5–6, SV 1419023608

Name _____ Date _____

Making Food Choices

People choose the foods they eat for many reasons. Understanding why people choose certain foods can help you make healthful food choices. Sometimes people select a food because their families or friends like that food. Where people live can also influence their food choices. Many families have come to the United States from other countries. Often these families choose the same foods they ate before coming to the United States. Sometimes people choose a food because it reminds them of a happy time. People may also select particular foods because they are plentiful, in season, familiar, or have a reasonable price. People may also choose a type of food because of an advertisement.

 Read the paragraph above. Use this information to help you complete the activity below.

In the first column of the table, list four foods and one drink you would like to have at a meal. In the second column, name the food group or food groups to which each food belongs. In the third column, write the reason or reasons you like each food. You may use another health book if you need help.

My Favorite Meal	Food Group(s)	Why I Like That Food
1.		
2.		
3.		
4.		
5.		

Being a Vegetarian

You've probably heard about **vegetarians**, but you may not know exactly what being a vegetarian means. Someone who is a vegetarian eats no meat of any kind. That means eating no flesh of any animal, including chicken and fish.

People usually follow a vegetarian diet for one of two reasons—either for moral reasons or for health concerns. Many people feel that it's not right to eat other animals. They may also feel that eating meat is a wasteful practice when so many people in the world do not have enough to eat. This reasoning is based on the fact that cattle are fed grain that could be used to feed people. As you know from reading about food webs, energy is lost as it goes from one living thing to the next. In other words, a cow takes in much more energy than a human or another animal could gain from eating its flesh.

Many people follow a vegetarian diet because of health concerns. A vegetarian diet is one way of lowering the amount of fat a person eats. A meat-centered diet is often very high in fat, and high-fat diets have been shown to be a factor in many diseases, including heart disease and cancer.

Some vegetarians avoid not only meat but also animal products, such as eggs and milk. This diet is harder to follow because many foods, from breads to salads, may contain ingredients made from milk or eggs. Other vegetarians believe it is okay to eat animal products as long as the animal is not harmed. These people get protein from foods such as yogurt, cottage cheese, and other milk products. Some vegetarians also eat products that contain eggs.

Vegetarians who eat egg and milk products can easily get enough protein, an important part of a healthful diet. Those who do not eat any eggs or milk must be more careful to make sure they get enough protein in their diets. Many foods, such as beans, nuts, and grains, have high levels of protein. A variety of these foods must be eaten together to provide the proteins the body needs to stay healthy. Eating beans and rice together provides this kind of protein.

Answer these questions.

1. What is a vegetarian? _____

   _____

2. Why might it be more healthful to be a vegetarian than to eat a traditional American diet?

   _____

   _____

3. Suggest a menu for a vegetarian meal. If you like, it may contain milk and egg products.

   _____

Name _____ Date _____

Food Safety

 Read the paragraphs. Then answer the questions.

Rachel likes to help her father in the kitchen. On Monday, she decided she would make Tuesday's lunches. She took out turkey, mayonnaise, and bread for sandwiches, and placed the items on the counter. She made the sandwiches, wrapped them in plastic wrap, and left them on the counter so she and her dad would see them the next morning. Then she placed the turkey and the mayonnaise back in the refrigerator and placed the unused slices of bread back in their package.

Rachel also made a small fruit salad. She took some strawberries and two oranges from the refrigerator. She cut the stems from the strawberries and sliced them. She peeled the oranges and divided them into sections. Next, she mixed up the fruit and divided the mixture into two airtight plastic containers. She placed the containers on the counter next to the sandwiches.

1. Name three things Rachel did that show she was thinking about food safety.

_____

_____

_____

_____

2. Name three things Rachel did not do that she should have done.

_____

_____

_____

_____

3. Write two or more sentences that tell what might happen next and why.

_____

_____

_____

_____

_____

Health, Nutrition, and P.E. 5–6, SV 1419023608

Name _____ Date _____

Preparing Healthful Foods

 Read the following paragraphs. As you read, take notes about the important facts.

Foods that are prepared in healthful ways can also be delicious. **Stir-frying** is one way to reduce the amount of fat in foods. When you stir-fry foods, you use only a small amount of vegetable oil. **Steaming** is even better. Steaming cooks foods without bringing the foods into contact with water, which can remove nutrients. Another way to cook foods without using fat is to cook them in a microwave oven.

Fruits and vegetables make delicious snacks, but they should always be washed before they are eaten. Washing removes dirt, harmful **microbes**, and **insecticides**. To help preserve the nutrients in fruits and vegetables, eat them raw or cook them only until they are tender. Steaming vegetables preserves many more nutrients than does boiling.

Seasoning can be added to foods to give them additional flavor. Careful use of seasoning can help you avoid using too much salt, which can cause a person's blood pressure to rise. To sweeten foods, consider alternatives to sugar. For example, adding fruit to foods such as cereal will sweeten them naturally and keep them nutritious.

Notes:

To avoid cooking foods in a lot of fat

1. _____

2. _____

3. _____

Get the most out of the fruits and vegetables you eat by

4. _____

5. _____

To add flavor to foods without using a lot of salt or sugar

6. _____

7. _____

Unit 3: Physical Education
Teacher Resource

To be fit, a person must have good muscle tone and must not be markedly overweight or underweight. Physical activity can help to tone most muscles, but aerobic exercise is necessary to tone the heart muscle. In addition, calorie intake must be balanced with calorie burning so that an acceptable weight is maintained.

Exercising has many healthful benefits. First, muscles grow when they are used. Unexercised muscles contract when they are not used. Muscles that become unaccustomed to exercise can be injured by sudden or strenuous activity. This is why muscles, including the heart, should be exercised regularly and in moderation. Occasional strenuous activity is not advantageous to the muscles and does not give long-term results.

Moreover, exercise also controls weight and increases endurance and strength. Regular exercise can also relax the body, reduce stress, and help people get a good night's sleep. Finally, exercise can reduce the rate of premature mortality, including heart disease, hypertension, and colon cancer.

Since schools are often financially restricted, the physical education curriculum is considered less important. The classroom teacher must provide rich and varied experiences for students so they can exercise as well as learn how to establish and maintain a healthy lifestyle. Teachers are responsible for developing a wide variety of activities that promote basic movement skills; games for individuals, partners, and teams; physical fitness; and dance. Teachers also need to ensure that each student achieves his or her optimum mental, emotional, social, and physical development. This is a tall order when the curriculum is already packed with the need to teach core subjects.

The pages in this unit deal with burning calories and establishing fitness goals. The later pages deal with physical skills in popular sports. Pages 91 and 92 give specific instructions on how to shoot, dribble, and pass a basketball so that students can gain and practice the skills more readily. Page 93 also gives specific instructions on how to pass a football.

Track and field events require little equipment and produce good physical activity. The same is true for basketball and kickball. The main focus of any physical activity program is to get the students moving so they can burn those calories. The activities can be set up as competitions among students or as noncompetitive events where students judge their own individual improvement over a period of time.

Health, Nutrition, and P.E. 5–6, SV 1419023608

Bulletin Board: Burn Those Calories!

Burn Those Calories!

A Person Who Weighs 115 Pounds Burns This Many Calories

Activity	Calories Burned in 30 Minutes
Sitting Still	31
Raking Leaves	86
Walking on a Sidewalk	124
Bicycling (10 mph)	160
Mowing the Lawn	176
Swimming Fast	260
Running (9-minute mile)	300

A bulletin board for physical activities should center on burning calories.

Teacher Directions

1. Include this information on your bulletin board:
   - To maintain a current weight, a person must burn as many calories as he or she takes in.
   - To lose weight, a person must burn more calories than he or she intakes.
   - A student at this grade level should intake about 1,800 to 2,200 calories per day.
2. Include the question: How many calories do you burn each day?
3. Construct a chart for the bulletin board. It should look like the one above.
4. Include students' pictures around the bulletin board.

Student Directions

1. Select an activity from the list on the bulletin board.
2. Choose one day of the week and do that activity.
3. After you have done the activity, draw a picture of yourself doing it.
4. Repeat for as many activities as you like.

Health, Nutrition, and P.E. 5–6, SV 1419023608

Burning Calories

When you eat food, you take in calories. When you do physical activities, you burn calories. To maintain a current weight, a person must burn as many calories as he or she takes in. To lose weight, a person must burn more calories than he or she takes in.

 Complete the chart. For each physical activity, multiply your weight by the number in the Per Pound column. This gives you calories burned per minute. Then multiply calories burned per minute by the number of minutes shown in the other columns.

Calories Burned During Physical Activities

Activity	Per Pound	Calories Burned per Minute	Calories Burned in 15 Minutes	Calories Burned in 30 Minutes	Calories Burned in 60 Minutes
Sitting Still	0.009				
Sleeping	0.010				
Cooking	0.022				
Grocery Shopping	0.028				
Biking (6 mph)	0.027				
Jumping Rope	0.083				
Running in Place	0.072				
Walking (3 mph)	0.036				
Tennis (singles)	0.044				
Aerobic Dancing	0.060				

Use the chart to answer the questions.

1. How many calories would you burn sitting still for an hour? _____

2. How many calories would you burn sleeping for 8 hours? _____

3. Which of the activities in the chart do you do? _____

_____

4. Do you think you take in or burn more calories each day? _____

_____

Health, Nutrition, and P.E. 5–6, SV 1419023608

Name _____   Date _____

Set Your Fitness Goals

ᗡᗡᗡᗡᗡᗡᗡᗡᗡᗡᗡᗡᗡᗡᗡᗡᗡᗡᗡᗡᗡᗡᗡᗡᗡᗡᗡᗡᗡᗡᗡᗡᗡ

 Read the paragraph. Then answer the questions.

> Karen will be staying at her aunt's apartment in the city for a week while her parents are away on vacation. She enjoys being with her aunt, but she is afraid she will have difficulty sticking to her fitness plan. She won't be able to do her regular activities, such as bike riding on country roads. How can she use the following goal-setting steps to make sure she gets her 30 minutes of daily exercise while away?

Step 1: Set a goal. What goal could Karen set?

_____

_____

Step 2: List steps to reach that goal.
What steps could Karen take to reach her goal?

_____

_____

Step 3: Monitor progress toward the goal.
How could Karen monitor her progress?

_____

_____

_____

Step 4: Evaluate your progress.
How could Karen evaluate her progress?

_____

What other benefits would Karen receive from meeting this goal?

_____

_____

Health, Nutrition, and P.E. 5–6, SV 1419023608

How Fit Are You?

Exercising has many healthful benefits. First, muscles grow when they are used. Unexercised muscles contract when they are not used. Muscles that are not accustomed to exercise can be injured by sudden or strenuous activity. This is why muscles, including the heart, should be exercised regularly. Occasional strenuous activity is not helpful to the muscles and does not give long-term results.

Exercise also helps you to control your weight and increase your endurance and strength. Regular exercise can relax your body, reduce stress, and help you to get a good night's sleep. Finally, exercise can help you to live longer and to prevent diseases such as heart disease, high blood pressure, and colon cancer.

If you exercise regularly, you can keep your muscles strong and your body healthy. Bodies that are physically fit have four important characteristics: they are strong, flexible, well-coordinated, and can endure exercise over a long period of time.

 Do these tests to see how fit you are. Wear loose clothes and gym shoes.

1. Are your arms and shoulders strong?

Flexed-Arm Hang

Using an overhand grip, hang with your chin above the bar and with your elbows flexed. Keep your legs straight and feet free of the floor.

To pass: Hold at least 3 seconds.

My score: _____

Pull-ups

Using an overhand grip, hang with your arms and legs fully extended, feet free of the floor. Pull your body up until your chin is higher than the bar. Lower your body until your arms are fully extended. Keep pull-ups smooth and don't kick your legs.

To pass: Do at least 1 pull-up.

My score: _____

Go on to the next page.

How Fit Are You?, p. 2

2. Are your abdominal muscles strong?

Sit-ups

Do this exercise with a partner. Lie on your back with knees flexed, feet one foot apart. With fingers laced, grasp your hands behind your head. Have a partner hold your ankles and keep your heels in contact with the floor. Sit up and touch your right elbow to the left knee. Return to the starting position. Then, sit up and touch your left elbow to the right knee.

To pass: Check the chart.

Age	Amount of Exercise
10	25 sit-ups
11	26 sit-ups
12	30 sit-ups

My score: _____

3. Are you well-coordinated?

Squat Thrusts

Stand straight. On count 1, bend your knees and place your hands on the floor. On count 2, thrust your legs back so your body is in a push-up position. On count 3, return to a squat position. On count 4, return to a standing position. Do as many as you can in 10 seconds.

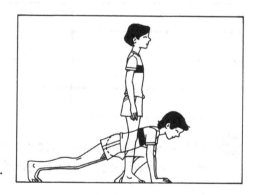

To pass: You should do at least 4 squat thrusts in 10 seconds.

My score: _____

How fit are you? _____

_____

_____

_____

Health, Nutrition, and P.E. 5–6, SV 1419023608

My Fitness Goal Log

Choose a personal fitness goal for the next 30 days. Be sure your goal is specific, including the following details:
- activities you will do;
- days you will work out;
- number of minutes for your workouts.

 Record your progress daily in a chart like the following.

Day	Activity	How many	Number of minutes

After 30 days, monitor your progress to see how much improvement you've made. Answer the questions.

1. Are you able to do more of each activity now than when you began?

   _____

2. Do you feel more fit now?

   _____

3. What are some of the benefits of being fit?

   _____

   _____

86

Name _____ Date _____

How Does Exercise Change Your Pulse Rate?

Materials

a clock or a watch with a second hand

Procedure

1. Stand up for two minutes. While standing, hold your fingers in the correct position for feeling your pulse. Ask a helper to signal the beginning and end of one minute. Find your pulse rate. Record it in the chart.
2. Lie down for two minutes. Then, take your pulse rate, and record it in the chart.
3. Sit up for two minutes. At the end of two minutes, take your pulse rate. Record it in the chart.
4. Run in place for one minute. As soon as you stop, take your pulse rate. Record it in the chart.

Situation	Pulse rate
Standing	
Lying down	
Sitting	
After running	

Drawing Conclusions

1. When was your pulse rate the slowest?

   _____

2. When was your pulse rate the fastest?

   _____

3. Why does your pulse rate speed up when you exercise?

   _____

   _____

More Ideas for Your Project

- Try other activities to see how they affect your pulse rate, such as jumping rope or holding your breath for one minute.
- Do research on pulse rates. What rates are considered normal for people of different ages?

Health, Nutrition, and P.E. 5–6, SV 1419023608

Warm Up and Cool Down

Have you ever been to a football game? Do you remember seeing the players warm up? Cold, tight muscles should be warmed up and stretched little by little. This prevents muscle injuries and muscle soreness. There are two types of warm-ups. General warm-ups are for the whole body. These exercises should take between three and five minutes. They should include some stretching, some calisthenics (like jumping jacks), and some walking and jogging. There are also specific warm-ups. These exercises help the body get ready for the sport. For example, in softball, players may throw the ball back and forth.

Cool-down exercises are just as important as warm-ups. Cool-down exercises take about ten minutes. You should gradually slow down your activity. For example, cool down after jogging by walking. Stretching should also be part of the cool-down exercises. This can prevent muscle soreness.

 Make a list of sports or athletics that you engage in. In the other columns, make a list of warm-up and cool-down exercises you can do.

Sports	Warm Up	Cool Down

Health, Nutrition, and P.E. 5–6, SV 1419023608

Track Events

Most track events are foot races. Short foot races are called dashes or sprints. One of the most popular races in track meets is the 100-meter dash. You can start off with a shorter race.

50-Meter Dash and 100-Meter Dash

1. Set up beginning and ending cones or markers that are 50 meters apart. You will also need a stopwatch for each runner in a heat, or group of runners. For example, if four runners race at the same time, you will need four stopwatches and four people to operate the watches. Each person with a watch is assigned to time a specific runner.

2. The people with watches wait at the ending marker. The runners and the starter wait by the beginning marker. When the starter shouts "Go!" the runners start racing. The people with watches also start the watches. When a timer's specific runner crosses the end line, the timer stops the watch.

3. The beginning and ending markers can be set 100 meters apart for a longer race.

   My time in the 50-meter dash: _____

   My time in the 100-meter dash: _____

Relay Race

1. In a relay race, four runners are on a team. Each runner races a specific length, then passes a baton or stick to the next runner on the team. After all four runners have raced, the team score is the time it took all four runners to complete the race. Usually two or three teams will run at once.

2. Set up beginning and ending cones or markers that are 50 meters apart. You will need a stopwatch for each team of runners. You will also need something for each team of runners to pass on to their teammates as the relay race continues. You can use a tennis ball, for example, or a short stick.

3. The starter, the timers, and two members of each team wait by the beginning marker. A judge and the other two members wait at the ending marker. When the starter says "Go!" the timers start the stopwatches and the first member of each team runs to the ending marker. When he or she passes the marker, the tennis ball is given to the next runner on the team. That runner then races to the beginning marker and gives the ball to the next runner on the team. The relay continues until all runners have completed their leg of the race. The timer for each team stops the watch when the last member of the team crosses the end line, which will be by the beginning marker.

4. Each runner must run past the marker before passing on the ball. If the ball is dropped, the runner must pick it up before he or she can continue the race.

5. Compare race times after everyone has run the race.

   My team's time in the relay race: _____

Name _____ Date _____

Field Events

Most field events involve jumping or throwing. On this page, you will learn about several field events that you can try.

Broad Jump

1. The broad jump, or long jump, is a contest to leap the farthest distance along the ground. The distance is measured from a starting line to the point the jumper's body touches the ground closest to the starting line. For example, if the jumper hits the ground and falls forward, the distance would be from the starting line to the point the most rearward foot hit the ground. If the jumper hits the ground and falls backward, the distance would be from the starting line to the point the jumper's hand or body hit the ground. Distances can be measured in feet or meters. Jumpers jump one at a time. Judges should stand nearby to mark where each jumper's body hits.
2. Mark a starting line on the ground. If possible, make marks on the ground every foot or meter from the starting line. You will need a long measuring tool to get an accurate distance for each jump.
3. In the standing broad jump, the jumper stands with both feet behind the starting line. Then, the jumper jumps forward, and the distance is measured.
4. In the running broad jump, the jumper can run any distance before jumping at the starting line. However, the jumper must jump before his or her foot crosses the starting line. Then, the jumper jumps forward, and the distance is measured.
5. Compare jump distances after everyone has jumped.

My distance in the standing broad jump: _____

My distance in the running broad jump: _____

Softball Throw

1. In the softball throw, the contestant throws the ball for distance. The ball can be thrown underhand or overhand.
2. Mark a starting line on the ground. If possible, make marks on the ground every 10 feet or 3 meters from the starting line. You will need a long measuring tool to get an accurate distance for each throw. Judges should stand in the field ready to mark where each ball hits.
3. Each person throws one at a time. The distance is measured from the starting line to the point the ball first hits the ground.
4. Compare throw distances after everyone has thrown.

My distance in the underhand softball throw: _____

My distance in the overhand softball throw: _____

Basketball Skills

Playing basketball uses many skills. Players have to run, jump, pass, and shoot. On this page, you will be able to test several of your basketball skills.

Dribbling

1. The basic basketball skill is **dribbling**. In basketball, you can only advance the ball by dribbling it or passing it. When you dribble, your hand should be slightly cupped and always above the ball. You will use your hand and wrist more to dribble than your arm. Push down on the ball with your fingers. The ball will spring back to your fingers. Do not catch the ball, but push it back down to the floor. You are dribbling. Count how many times you dribble the ball without stopping. Can you dribble with your eyes closed? Give it a try.

2. Now, start moving forward while dribbling the ball. Remember, you can't hold or carry the ball. Your hand should always be above the ball while you are dribbling. When you stop dribbling, you must stop and pass or shoot. You cannot start dribbling again.

Number of times I could dribble the ball: _____

Number of times I could dribble the ball with my eyes closed: _____

Number of steps I could take while dribbling the ball: _____

Shooting Free Throws

1. In all levels of basketball, the free-throw line is 15 feet from the hoop. Being a good free-throw shooter requires focus, accuracy, and practice. There are several ways to attempt the shot.

2. One way is to shoot **underhand**, which is also known as the **granny shot**. Stand behind the middle of the free-throw line. Spread your hands under the ball. Let the ball rest in your hands. Spread your legs, bend your knees, and bring the ball back between your knees. As you come up, roll the ball off your fingertips toward the basket. The ball should be spinning away from you. This motion of the ball is called **topspin**.

3. You can also hold the ball on the sides. As you come up using this **grip**, move your fingers up and around the front of the ball. You want the ball to be spinning toward you as it leaves your hands. This motion of the ball is called bottom spin, or **backspin**. Try both spins. Which works better for you?

4. Another way is to shoot **overhand**. In this shot, you cup your shooting hand a bit and rest it on the back of the ball. Your other hand is on the side to balance the ball. Your elbow should be close to your side. As your shooting arm moves up toward the basket, you release the other hand and push the ball. As you shoot, your forearm moves up and your wrist flicks forward.

5. Try both shooting styles. Which one is better for you? Remember, to become really good at some activity, you must practice, practice, practice.

My score for underhand free throws: _____

My score for overhand free throws: _____

Health, Nutrition, and P.E. 5–6, SV 1419023608

Name _____ Date _____

Basketball Skills, p. 2

The two ways to advance a basketball in a game are to dribble it or to pass it. There are two main types of basketball passes.

Chest Passes

1. The first kind of pass is the **chest pass**. Your hands should be to the back and sides of the ball. Bring the ball back to your chest. Your elbows should be pointed away to the sides of you. Push the ball away from you. When you finish the pass, your palms should be pointing outward. The ball should arrive at your partner at about the same spot it left your body.
2. Work with a partner. Use chest passes to move the basketball between you. Start passing at a distance of 5 feet. Make 3 passes back and forth at each distance. Then move to 10 feet, and on to 15 feet. How far can you chest-pass the ball without it hitting the ground?

Distance I can chest-pass in the air: _____

Bounce Passes

1. The second kind of pass is the **bounce pass**. As its name suggests, you bounce the ball in a bounce pass. When you bounce-pass, you want the ball to arrive at your partner's waist. To bounce-pass, you use the same passing movement as in the chest pass. Push the ball away from you toward the floor. When you finish the pass, your palms should be pointing outward.
2. Work with a partner. Use bounce passes to move the basketball between you. Start passing at a distance of 5 feet. Make 3 passes back and forth at each distance. Then move to 10 feet, and on to 15 feet. How far can you bounce-pass the ball with only one bounce?
3. Do you remember topspin and backspin? You can vary the distance your bounce pass travels using these spins. If you want your pass to go farther, use topspin. As you pass the ball, move your fingers over and around the top of the ball. Your thumbs will start under the ball and end up above the ball. The ball should be spinning away from you. A ball with topspin will bounce up lower to the ground.
4. You can also put backspin on the ball. Put your hands on the sides of the ball with your thumbs on top of it. Spin your thumbs back toward you and under the ball. If you put backspin on the ball, it will bounce up higher but somewhat stop in forward movement.

Distance I can bounce-pass with one bounce: _____

🍎 **Write complete sentences to answer the questions.**

1. What is the difference between topspin and backspin? _____

_____

2. What is probably the best way to improve any skill? _____

_____

Health, Nutrition, and P.E. 5–6, SV 1419023608

Throwing

A good thrower often has two skills: distance and accuracy. On this page, you can test your throwing skills in different ways.

Hit the Can

1. Set up a heavy trashcan in an open space. Each thrower should start 10 feet away from the trashcan. Have each person throw 10 tennis balls at the trashcan. A judge should count the number of balls that land in the trashcan. Bounces do not count. Throwers may use the overhand or underhand grip.

2. Then the throwers should move to 15 or 20 feet away from the trashcan. Again, have each person throw 10 balls at the trashcan. Continue to move farther away from the trashcan.

Number of balls I hit from 10 feet: _____

Number of balls I hit from 15 feet: _____

Number of balls I hit from 20 feet: _____

Football Toss

1. A good football passer must be able to hit still and moving targets. There are many ways to throw a football. Here is one way. Grip the football with your fingertips on the laces and your thumb under the ball. As you bring the ball back, it will pass close to your head. The elbow of your throwing arm will be pointing away from your body. When you throw the football, you straighten your arm and spin your hand under the ball. When you finish the throw, your arm should be pointing toward your target, and your fingers should be pointing that way, too. But now your thumb is pointing up.

2. Work with a partner. Move 15 feet apart and start throwing the ball to each other. Are your throws accurate? Does the ball spin smoothly or does it wobble? Remember, practice, practice, practice. How far can you and your partner throw the ball accurately?

3. Now work on a pass play with your partner. The receiver will run about 15 feet and turn left or right. The passer will throw the ball to the spot the receiver should be. The receiver should catch the ball while moving, not while standing still. After 5 attempts, the passer becomes the receiver.

Distance I could throw the football in the air: _____

Distance I could throw the football accurately in the air: _____

Number of caught passes I threw in the pass play: _____

Number of passes I caught in the pass play: _____

Answer Key

Pages 5–7
1. D   11. B   21. B
2. A   12. A   22. A
3. B   13. B   23. A
4. A   14. C   24. D
5. C   15. C   25. C
6. C   16. C   26. C
7. D   17. B   27. D
8. B   18. D   28. D
9. C   19. D   29. A
10. A   20. C   30. C

Page 13
1. true   4. true
2. true   5. true
3. false   6. false
7. The two jobs of a cell are to take in food and give off wastes.

Page 14
1. holds small parts of the cell
2. tells the cells what its job is
3. lets food and wastes in and out of the cell
4. Nerve cells carry messages throughout the body.

Page 15
1. do not
2. cell
3. cells
4. skin
5. A tissue is a group of cells doing the same job.
6. The four kinds of body tissue are skin tissue, muscle tissue, nerve tissue, and connective tissue.

Page 16
1. true
2. false
3. true
4. false
5. false
6. tissues
7. an organ
8. organs

Page 17
1. C
2. B
3. A
4. E
5. D
6. Answers will vary.

Page 18
1. There are 206 bones in a skeleton.
2. The primary function of the skeletal system is to support and protect the soft tissues and organs of the body.
3. The three body parts that allow movement in many different ways are the bones, joints, and muscles.
4. Red marrow produces red blood cells, some white blood cells, and cell fragments. Red marrow can be found in the long bones of the body, as well as in the ribs, sternum, vertebrae, and pelvic bones.
5. Calcium and phosphorus are stored in bones.

Page 19
1. B   2. A   3. C   4. A

Page 20
1. true   4. false
2. false   5. true
3. true

Page 21
Across:
1. muscles
3. support
4. protect
Down:
2. skeletal
3. shape

Page 22
1. B   2. A   3. C   4. A

Page 23
1. voluntary
2. cardiac
3. smooth
4. skeletal

Page 24
1. Long, cylinder-shaped cells
2. Muscle cells that branch out and weave together. They make up the heart.
3. Long, thin, and pointed cells
4.–6. Check students' drawings.

Page 25
1. involuntary, cardiac
2. voluntary, skeletal
3. involuntary, smooth
4. involuntary, smooth
5. involuntary, smooth
6. voluntary, skeletal
7. involuntary, smooth
8. voluntary, skeletal

Page 26
1. Answers will vary.
2. One arm is used more than the other. The more exercise the muscles get, the better the muscle tone.
3. push-ups, weight lifting, etc.
4. It would be easier to improve the tone of your voluntary muscles because you can exercise them.

Page 27
1. oxygen
2. heart
3. carbon dioxide
4. cell
5. blood

Page 28
1. An artery carries blood away from the heart.
2. A vein returns blood to the heart.
3. Body cells get food and oxygen from capillaries.

Page 29
Answers will vary but should suggest that a healthy heart makes a person more healthy and active overall.

Page 30
1. heart   6. 3
2. artery   7. 5
3. capillaries   8. 2
4. vein   9. 1
5. lungs   10. 4

Page 31
1. B   2. C   3. D   4. A

Page 32
Across:
4. respiratory
6. lungs
7. windpipe
8. nose
Down:
1. diaphragm
2. bronchial
3. diffusion
5. sac

Page 33
1. Responses will vary but may include the fact that respiration rate increases with activity.
2. The respiration rate increases.

Page 34
1. A burning candle uses up the oxygen.
2. The longer the breath was held, the shorter the time the candle burned.
3. The longer you hold your breath, the less oxygen and the more carbon dioxide you will exhale.

Page 35
1. The two functions of the digestive system are to break food into nutrients and to get the nutrients into the blood.
2. The four main organs of the digestive system are the mouth, the stomach, the small intestine, and the large intestine.
3. Saliva is a liquid in the mouth that changes starch into sugar.

Health, Nutrition, and P.E. 5–6, SV 1419023608

Answer Key continued

Page 36
1. C 2. B 3. D 4. A

Page 37
1. Answers will vary.
2. It should taste sweet. An enzyme in saliva has changed some of the starch to sugar.
3. Chew them. If they contain starch, they will taste sweet after a bit.
4. Check students' responses.

Page 38
1. waste
2. rectum
3. bacteria
4. true
5. true

Page 39
1. B 2. C 3. D 4. A
5. The body would become infected because it would not function properly.

Page 40
1. The central nervous system is made up of the brain and spinal cord. The peripheral nervous system is made up of the sensory organs.
2. A neuron is a special cell that can receive and transmit nerve signals.
3. A reflex is an automatic muscle response.

Page 41
1. A 2. D 3. B 4. C

Page 42
1. true   4. true
2. false   5. true
3. false

Page 43
The answers are in the following order: 2, 5, 1, 4, 6, 3.

Page 44
1. touch, temperature, pain, pressure
2. Answers may vary. There are more nerve endings in the fingers because the fingers help us learn about our world through touch.
3. The person would get burned.

Page 45
1. taste buds
2. taste nerves
3. brain
4. bitter

Page 46
1. words
2. numbers
3. facts
4. visual patterns
5. imagination
6. math teachers
7. artists

Page 47
1. The uncut apple stayed fresh, or started to decay after several days. The cut apple decayed quickly. The skin of the uncut apple protected the apple from things that could harm it.
2. The skin of the apple protects it from harmful things. The skin of a person will keep harmful things, like disease, from entering the body, too.

Page 48
1. The function of hormones is to control different activities in the body.
2. Target tissues are tissues affected by hormones secreted by the endocrine glands.
3. The target tissue of the pancreas is the liver.
4. The thyroid gland regulates metabolism, energy levels, and growth and development of the body.

Page 49
1. hormones
2. pituitary gland
3. glands
4. Adrenalin
5. puberty
6. ovaries

Page 50
1. B 2. C 3. A 4. A

Page 51
1. pregnant
2. 9 months
3. blood vessels
4. placenta
5. navel

Page 52
1. true
2. false
3. true
4. false
5. true
6.–7. Sentences will vary.

Page 53
1. T   5. F   9. F
2. F   6. F   10. F
3. T   7. F
4. T   8. T

Page 54
Answers will vary.

Page 55
Answers will vary.

Page 56
1. false   4. true
2. false   5. true
3. true   6. false

Page 57
1. Answers may vary but could include: It increases heartbeat, produces a cough, makes breathing difficult. It destroys vitamins. It leads to diseases of the circulatory and respiratory systems.
2. Answers may vary but could include: Their friends smoke. They want to look older.

Page 58
1. Price will vary but should be realistic.
2. cost per pack × 365
3. cost per year × 40 years
4. 20 × 365 = 7,300
5. 7,300 × 40 = 292,000
6. 292,000 × 5.5 = 1,606,000
7. 1,606,000 divided by 60 = 26,767 hours; 26,767 divided by 24 = 1,115 days; 1,115 divided by 365 = 3 years
8. Answers will vary.

Page 60
Across:
2. fetal alcohol
3. absorb
4. BAC
7. hangover
Down:
1. alcoholism
5. cirrhosis
6. drunk

Page 61
1. F   3. D   5. A
2. C   4. E   6. B

Page 62
Answers may vary. Possible answers are given.
1. C; People should never take anyone else's prescription medicines. Since Clara's family has no way of knowing whether the OTC medicines are free from germs or contamination, they should throw them away also.
2. C; Self-medication can be dangerous for everyone, but it is especially dangerous for children.

Page 63
Answers will vary.

Pages 67–71
Check students' work on the web site.

Health, Nutrition, and P.E. 5–6, SV 1419023608

Answer Key *continued*

Page 72
1. D   3. A   5. C
2. F   4. B   6. E
7. Possible answers:
   carbohydrates—bread,
   spaghetti, candy; fats—
   butter, ice cream, cooking
   oils; protein—meat, fish,
   eggs, cheese; vitamins—
   vegetables, milk, fruits,
   cereals; minerals—all
   foods; water—water, juice

Page 73
Answers will vary.

Page 74
1. yes
2. A black spot appeared on
   them.

Page 75
1. 120 without milk; 190
   with milk
2. carbohydrates
3. sugar
4. Recommended Daily
   Allowance
5. 25%
6. calcium, iron, phosphorus,
   magnesium, zinc, copper
7. wheat bran, raisins,
   sugar, salt, malt flavoring
   (Ingredients are listed in
   order of amounts.)
8. Increase protein by adding
   whole milk.

Page 76
Answers will vary.

Page 77
1. A vegetarian is a person
   who eats no meat. Some
   do not drink milk or eat
   animal products either.
2. A vegetarian diet is usually
   much lower in fat. High-
   fat diets are a health risk.
3. Answers will vary.

Page 78
1. She wrapped the
   sandwiches in plastic;
   she put the fruit salad
   in airtight containers;
   she put the turkey and
   mayonnaise back into
   the refrigerator when she
   was done preparing the
   sandwiches.
2. She did not wash the
   counter before she started;
   she did not wash the
   strawberries; she did not
   refrigerate the sandwiches
   or the fruit salad.
3. Rachel and her father may
   get food poisoning. Germs
   from the unrefrigerated
   meat, the counter, and
   the unwashed fruit
   could multiply. Germs
   grow rapidly at room
   temperature.

Page 79
1. stir-fry foods
2. steam foods
3. cook foods in a microwave
   oven
4. washing them first
5. eating them raw or
   cooking them only until
   tender
6. use seasonings instead of
   salt
7. substitute other sweeteners
   for sugar, such as fresh
   fruit

Page 82
Answers will vary. Check
students' calculations.

Page 83
Answers will vary. Accept
reasonable responses. Possible
answers are given.
1. Her goal is to get 30
   minutes of exercise daily
   while visiting her aunt.
2. Karen could ask her aunt
   to go with her on a brisk
   walk daily or join her aunt
   at the local gym when her
   aunt does her workout.
3. She could record her daily
   exercise (brisk walk or
   gym workout) for a week
   on a calendar.
4. She could check the
   calendar to see how she is
   doing.
Other benefits: She'll enjoy
time with her aunt and feel
more comfortable in the city.

Pages 84–85
Check students' results.

Page 86
Answers will vary. Check
students' charts.

Page 87
Check students' results.
Answers may vary.
1. when sitting still or lying
   down
2. after running in place
3. Exercise makes the heart
   beat faster to supply the
   extra energy.

Page 88
Answers will vary. Check
students' charts.

Pages 89–93
Check students' results.

Health, Nutrition, and P.E. 5–6, SV 1419023608

4500685684
Printed in the United States of America